A Route Map to Novel Writing Success

Luscious Books

David Hough was born in Cornwall and grew up in the Georgian City of Bath. He spent forty years working as an air traffic controller in Northern Ireland, Scotland and England before retiring early in 2003 and becoming a writer. David has written over 30 novels and enjoys writing "a rattling good yarn with a dose of hard grit". He now lives with his wife in Dorset, on the south coast of England.

www.TheNovelsofDavidHough.com

Books by David Hough:

Non-fiction:

A Route Map to Novel Writing Success:
How to Write a Novel Using the Waypoint Method

A Route Map to Novel Writing Success: The Workbook
A Practical Aid to Using the Waypoint Method

Fiction:

Danger in the Sky aviation thrillers
Prestwick
Heathrow

Secret Soldiers of World War I spy thrillers
In Foreign Fields
In Line of Fire

Historical Adventures in Cornwall series
In the Shadow of a Curse
In the Shadow of Disgrace
In the Shadow of Deception

The Family Legacy series
The Legacy of Shame
The Legacy of Secrets
The Legacy of Conflict

A Route Map to Novel Writing Success

How to Write a Novel Using the Waypoint Method

David Hough

Published by Luscious Books Ltd 2017
Morwellham, Down Park Drive, Tavistock, PL19 9AH, Great Britain

ISBN 978-1-910929-07-0

A CIP catalogue record for this book is available from the British Library.

www.lusciousbooks.co.uk

The contents

INTRODUCTION

There is a saying within literary circles that 'everyone has a book within them... and that's where most of them should stay'. There is some doubt about who was the first to come up with the witticism, but that's not important. What is important is the meaning behind it: most people are *not skilled* in the art of writing books. And why should they be when they have not been taught how to go about it? But here's the good news: new novelists *can* be taught the best techniques, and they *can* become skilled in the art of writing.

I have attended numerous writers' classes, seminars and conferences where I have met new writers who would like to produce a novel, but they don't know how to begin. Some have written short stories, but there is a big difference between that and producing a full-length novel. I have heard many reasons why people struggle with novel writing, including:

"I'd like to write a novel, but I simply don't know where to start."

"I have this idea for a novel, but I've no idea how to go about writing it. I'm worried about getting it all wrong."

"The thought of tackling such a long piece of writing scares me."

There are many more reasons why potential novelists have given up before they have even started. That's a pity because the task isn't rocket science. I believe that the majority of these people *could* have written a book if only they had been taught how to construct their stories and had been encouraged to overcome their fears of planning and getting through the process of writing such a lengthy piece of work.

You don't need a university degree. I have met successful novelists who, for one reason or another, ended their schooling early without any formal qualifications. It was only in later life that they made the effort to learn the techniques of story writing. Which serves to confirm my belief that, although writing a novel is demanding in respect of time and effort, the basic techniques can be learned.

And that's what this book is all about.

There are numerous other books on the market aimed at showing people how to write a novel. I've read many of them. They were all written by published novelists, and so is this one. So, what makes this particular book different?

1. It makes no prior assumptions about your current writing skills. If you have never attempted to write a novel, this book will take you through a step-by-step process that works for me time and again. I can't categorically promise it will work for you — that would be foolish — but the odds are high that it will.

2. In preparing this book, I drew upon my wide experience as a qualified Trainer of Trainers. I am not just a novelist. In my previous career I was well qualified in teaching techniques. I wrote books on those techniques for my employers. I wrote film scripts for instructor-

training courses. And I held down a job teaching others how to teach. That's why this book will take you through the planning process in a logical manner.

3. The book will concentrate upon techniques that will help you avoid wasted effort. Even experienced novelists can — and do — sometimes come up against a brick wall and have to start again. That sort of waste is not inevitable. This book will show you valuable techniques that will give you the confidence of knowing, right from the start, that your story will work. You should not have to scrap thousands of words because they are going nowhere.

4. The text will include real examples taken from my own novels. Examples are always useful, but we should always be a little wary of examples taken from other writers' works. I will use one or two, but can I ever be totally sure what was in those other writers' minds? You can be sure of what was in my mind because I will tell you.

So, forget about your fears of getting it wrong or not being able to finish your novel. This manual will lead you towards a successful conclusion. If you adhere to the guidance that follows, you will have a very good chance of ending up with a well-constructed book.

My background

I have already mentioned my experience as a trainer, but that doesn't, by itself, make me a novelist. So, what right have I to show you how to write a novel? Let me give you a little more background information about myself.

I spent forty years working as an air traffic controller, which couldn't be much further removed from the job of a novelist. It was, however, a useful experience in many ways and I continue to draw novel-writing ideas from that time.

I then went on to become a training officer and learned valuable teaching techniques which helped youngsters follow in my footsteps. After many years of daily sweat and toil, I became a Trainer of Trainers, as I have already mentioned. I had to plan and run courses on behalf of my employers and I used a *systems approach* that ensured everything worked the way I wanted it to work. Those courses were successful because of the systematic way they were designed.

What is important here is that I learned how to teach and how to use that step-by-step systematic approach to good effect. I'm now going to teach you all I have learned about writing novels.

I didn't actually retire when I stopped working as an air traffic controller. Instead, I changed my career and became a writer. This was when my previous experience put me a step ahead of the game. I turned to what I had learned when using that systematic approach to training. It enabled me to devise a step-by-step system for writing novels, one that worked *because it was designed to work, right from the outset.* The step-by-step approach — which I have named the *Waypoint Method* — enabled me to write novel after novel and get them published. At the time of writing this manual, I have had over thirty novels published in the UK and North America. I have no rejected manuscripts lurking away in a bottom drawer. If my system works for me, it could work for you.

Why do you want to write a novel?

A publisher once told me, "For every thousand novels that are started, only one will be completed. For every thousand novels that are completed, only one will be of marketable quality." Harsh words, but they have a very important message, and it is this: the vast majority of potential novelists do not first learn how to do it.

That failure to first learn the techniques of writing stems, the publisher assured me, largely from the advent of the home computer. It's so easy to type out a stream of words and — almost instantly — see them nicely printed in a professional format. Those attractive-looking pages can give the writer a false impression: the impression that the story will be as good as the print quality. *And as easy to produce.*

Too many would-be novelists believe that, because they own a computer and printer, they can — without a great deal of bother — write a bestselling book. If only that were true!

The world of creative writing is littered with half-finished novels that will never be completed, and completed novels that no one wants to read because they are not good enough. Too many would-be writers spend months trying to create a literary masterpiece and end up in tears. But it doesn't have to end that way. You *can* write a viable novel with a good chance of being published if you go about it in the right way. And that's what I aim to show you as you work through the following pages.

From the fact that you have picked up this book, I can infer that you really do want to write a novel, and you want it to be a good one. You are a dedicated writer and you want to reach the last page of your manuscript with a smile on your face. But let's take a moment to first consider something you may have overlooked: *Why* do you want to write? Why do you want to spend months of your time — and it will take months, maybe years — in order to complete your first novel? Why do you want to expend all that creative power with no absolute guarantee that the end product will find a place on a publisher's list?

Is it because you want to make money out of writing? After all, published novelists make oodles of money, don't they? Well no, not all of them. Very few of them, in fact. And money isn't the only reason to write a novel. Some writers do it for the sheer pleasure of creating something new, and that's an admirable reason in itself. I can empathise with that approach. Most people, however, will probably want to do it to get published, one way or another.

That was *not* my starting point.

As I mentioned earlier, in my mortgage-paying days I was an air traffic controller. As high-pressure jobs go, it ranks well up the ladder. If a top brain surgeon makes one mistake, one patient could die. If an air traffic controller makes one mistake, a thousand people could die. It makes your eyes water just to think about it. I have worked alongside controllers who succumbed to stress-related illness or alcoholism before they reached the midpoint of their careers. I have worked alongside colleagues under pressure who died of a heart attack before they collected their pension.

My method of coping with the tensions of the job was — to start with — the relaxing pleasure of painting pictures. After a gruelling period on watch, I settled down at an easel and quietly painted away my stress. No one suggested or expected I should make money out of it. They recognised that I did it simply for the calm recreation it afforded me. Later, I took to writing for the same reason. Instead of creating pictures in oils, I created them in words. And it worked for me as a way of wiping away the bad after-effects of the job. I've had a love of books from my childhood so maybe it was a natural step for me to move from painting to writing.

In those early days I wrote short stories and I had a few published in magazines, but there was no prior intention to make money out of them. I wrote primarily as a way of calming my nerves.

Let me repeat something else that a publisher once told me. Most first novels, are not first novels. They are first *published* novels. Not the same thing. A publisher who bangs the drum for a brilliant first novel is often (deliberately) overlooking the writer's earlier, unpublished efforts which are now stacked away in a cupboard or drawer, gathering dust. The first abortive attempt at writing a novel — the one that's not fit for publication — is no major problem for the writer-for-pleasure, but it could be off-putting for the writer who is anxious to have his work widely read as quickly as possible, anxious to make a profit.

Such a writer might well question what's the point of writing a novel if there's no guarantee it will be published? The answer depends on why you choose to take up novel writing. Your book may not be published, but you can still have a printed copy sitting on your bookshelf.

A few months ago my grandson, Henry, said to me, "Grandad, will you write a book especially for me?" How could I refuse him? I did a lot of research into how children's books are written and then I wrote a short novel called *Henry the Ninth*. He was overjoyed to have a book that was written especially for him, and that gives me an enormous sense of satisfaction. There is only one printed copy, but one day, when I am long gone from this world, Henry will be reading that book to his children and his grandchildren. I have created something special for generations to come. Isn't that a good enough reason to write? Later, in the section on motivation, I will tell you more about why I continue to write now that I am retired from Air Traffic Control.

The technology of book production is, today, worlds ahead of what it was when I started writing. For a start, you can self-publish your book. You should be prepared for a steep learning curve if you choose this route, but it can be done by anyone with a little bit of internet knowhow and the willingness to learn.

Alternatively, you can upload your manuscript onto a website such as Lulu (www.lulu.com) and have a single copy printed in hardback or paperback, and it isn't expensive. If you want to write simply for the pure pleasure of writing, or for your family, go for it. Have a few copies printed and let your friends and relatives read them. Send out some copies as Christmas presents. Or bask in the pride of having the book on display in your home. There are many writers for whom this would be achievement enough.

This guidebook, however, is primarily aimed at helping you get published by a reputable publisher — again and again. If you have a different goal in mind, you can still use my Waypoint Method to finish your book. Just think positively and follow my step-by-step approach.

Different approaches to writing a novel

Two blokes go into a pub and one of them starts to tell the other about what happened down at the 'footie' ground last Saturday. He launches into a totally unprepared story of how his team beat the opposition two-nil. In his excitement, he doesn't relate the event as a well-structured tale, neatly thought out beforehand. Instead, he speaks off the cuff, just as the words come to his mind. Inevitably, there are moments of confusion because the story doesn't hang together in a cohesive form. The other bloke has to interrupt and say, "You mean it was Smith who headed in the first goal? But I thought you said...?"

The confusion arises because the story was not planned in advance. That's no problem for the two blokes in the pub — they can sort it out over a pint of beer — but is this how you want your novel to come across? Do you want to create a novel on the hoof, as you write it, with all the inherent risks? Some people do. Others, like me, plan the whole thing before they start to write.

All the novelists (published and unpublished) I have ever met — and they are many — can be roughly divided into three groups.

Firstly, there are those who diligently plan their novels from the start. I include myself in this group.

Secondly, there are those who start with a blank sheet of paper, or a blank computer screen, and make up the story as they go along. Rather like the bloke in the pub. We call them 'pantsers' because they 'fly by the seat of their pants' with no clear idea — to begin with — of where they are going. You'd be surprised how many new novelists use that approach to their writing. Even some experienced ones write that way. It can actually work, as I'll explain shortly, but it has some major pitfalls.

The third group? They're the ones who are not too sure which way they lean. They may do a bit of planning and then cast the plan aside when the muse starts to take them in a different direction. Or they may do a bit of pantsing, discover it's not working and try, belatedly, to formulate a plan to rescue the novel. It's usually too late by then. Or they may have some sort of unwritten plan in their heads, but no clear idea of how to put it into action. When asked, my advice to them is simple. If you feel inclined to be a planner, be a planner. If you feel inclined to be a pantser, be a pantser. But make up your mind and stick with your preferred style. In my experience of discussions with unpublished writers, a 'bit of each' rarely works well.

One successful writer I have known for many years is a committed pantser. She begins each new story with no preformed idea of what is going to happen or how it will all pan out, but she invariably gets there in the end. However, along the way she will often meet a brick wall. It's sometimes called 'writer's block'. Maybe the story doesn't seem to be going anywhere. Or maybe the characters she has devised are not in a position to take the story to a logical conclusion. Or maybe she began the whole story in the wrong place. Whatever the cause, at that point she will go back to the beginning and start again. That doesn't bother her unduly. It may entail scrapping twenty, thirty or forty thousand words, but she is willing to do that in order to get the story right. She is dedicated to her work and is willing to make such sacrifices. At the end of the day, she produces good novels and they sell. I admire her dedication.

Another writer, a good friend, is also a pantser. He totally rejects the idea of careful planning because — he says — it destroys his creativity. Fair enough. He's just had his first novel published so pantsing works for him. He is right to stick with it.

Pantsing works for those two authors. In a way. Many a

new writer, however, would be deterred by the risk of having to scrap so much hard-earned text when meeting the inevitable wall known as writer's block. I see it as a wasted effort, especially as it takes both of those writers noticeably longer than me to write a novel. That's why I prefer to plan my stories from the start. And that's why this book will concentrate upon the way planners, like myself, prefer to work.

I sometimes liken the job of novel writing to a shipyard building a brand new ocean liner. In the world of planners, the marine designers draw up a full set of blueprints before any metal is cut and, in consequence, everyone knows what should happen at each stage of the building process. If the shipyard was staffed by pantsers, however, things might work out quite differently. In a humorous vein, imagine how it would appear if they made it up as they went along. A couple of years later they might look at their new ship and say, "Yeah, it looks nice, but maybe we should have put the propellers at the back." That might be followed by, "Engines? Me? But I thought you were going to install the engines!"

In a similar vein, imagine how you'd feel if you spent a year of hard graft, slaving away night after night over your murder mystery novel and it all fell apart right at the end. When you offer your one hundred thousand words to a publisher, he says, "Yeah, it's nicely written, but you don't explain why the guy who did the murder in London was in Australia at the time. And why did the victim die on page two and then visit the hairdresser ten pages later?"

Back to the drawing board!

Don't get me wrong here. I reiterate what I wrote earlier: I'm not telling you that you must do it my way. If you think that pantsing is the best way for you to write a novel, you should tackle the task that way. The technique may actually work for you, but you should be aware of the risks you take. You may have to scrap thousands of hard-grafted words before you get to a satisfactory conclusion. Most pantsers meet up with that problem... *even if they never publicly admit to it.*

Bear in mind, also, the maxim: "If you know where your story started and you know where it is going, you will not get lost."

This is where I come to my first bit of myth-busting. The pantsers tell me — time and again — that instead of planning, they simply go with the flow because their stories are driven forward by their characters. "It's the characters who determine how the plot will progress," they assert.

"Nonsense," I reply. "The characters don't exist. They are figments of your imagination. It's your *imagination* that determines where the plot is going. And you have the ability to work with your imagination." Grab hold of that point and you are better placed to govern the plot and make it work for you.

My point is that writers — through the use of their imagination — can be in control of what a particular character may, or may not do. And here's another important point: one writer's determination about what happens next may be quite different to another writer's determination of what *exactly the same* character(s) may do in *exactly the same* situation. That is inevitable because no two writers will think in exactly the same way. Whichever way you look at it, the action is determined by the imagination of the writer, not the fictitious characters.

Let's look at that in a bit more depth. Not all of our thoughts and actions come from within our conscious minds. Some originate from within our subconscious minds. We may not be aware of what is lurking in the subconscious, but we cannot deny that it affects our behaviour and our thoughts. So, when you suddenly come up with a plot twist and you wonder where it came from, don't automatically ascribe it to the machinations of a fictitious character in your story. Don't say to yourself, "My character drove that plot forward." Instead, allow the fact that it came from your own subconscious thoughts which have been swirling around unseen in the darker reaches of your mind before elevating themselves into the conscious area of your brain.

It's now become a bit of an accepted myth that characters can be in control of driving forward the plot. Wrong. Keep telling yourself that it is your imagination that spurs on the plot and you can take control of that imagination once it is in the conscious area of your brain. The pantser will allow that imagination process to work in an uncontrolled way *while writing the novel* and will not consciously try to influence the direction in which it takes the story. That method of unplanned novel writing is fine until the story reaches the inevitable brick wall I mentioned earlier. Then it's back to the drawing board.

I prefer to let my imagination run riot *before* I start on Chapter 1. I play around with ideas, take heed of spurious thoughts and consider various options, long before I have written the opening sentence. I hold onto the bits of imagination that look good and discard the rest. It is only after my imagination has been given free rein, and the outcome consciously assessed in the early development process, that I will know exactly where I am going. I am consciously in control of my stories from the start.

I am a committed planner.

However, to reiterate an important point I made earlier: there isn't just one way to write a novel. If there was, it would have been set in concrete long before now.

Let me finish this section of the book with a confession. I

have tried pantsing. Just once. I have friends who are committed pantsers and they are sure their way is best. They adamantly tell me so. As a consequence, ten years ago I gave it a try. I started a novel with no clear idea where it was going. Twenty thousand words into the story I met a blank wall. The plot was now, belatedly, beginning to come together, but there was no way my key character could carry the emerging story to a satisfactory conclusion. He was an interesting character, but he was in the wrong story. It just wasn't going to work. Desperate to rescue the developing story, as it then was, I took advice from a professional source. I was told that the key character was wrong for that story, confirming what I already thought. And there was no way any amount of tweaking or fiddling with the manuscript could rectify the problem.

I had no alternative but to consign those twenty thousand words to the computer dustbin and start again. From that experience, I know how painful it is to scrap so much hard work. I started again from scratch and, this time, I went back to the way that works for me. I planned my story in advance. I designed a completely new key character who would be able to carry an amended plot to a satisfactory ending. Nothing from the original twenty thousand words was saved or re-used. I had to accept that there was nothing which could be reused. That newly-planned story worked. It was first published as *King's Priory.* When that publisher went bankrupt, two others came forward within a week and asked to take it (and my other books) on board. My current publisher has since released it as *The Legacy of Secrets.*

The Waypoint Method

I have already mentioned that I have a specific way of writing my novels that works for me every time and I call it the Waypoint Method. But what is this method exactly?

Think of your writing task as a journey, a long journey towards a distant destination. The Waypoint Method is a route map which will lead you towards your destination, a map marked out with specific points where you may stop and relax in the certain knowledge that you are on the right road to success. The method is based upon a very simple system that has worked well for me and enabled me to complete over thirty novels, all of which have been taken up by publishers.

Diagrammatically, it looks like this:

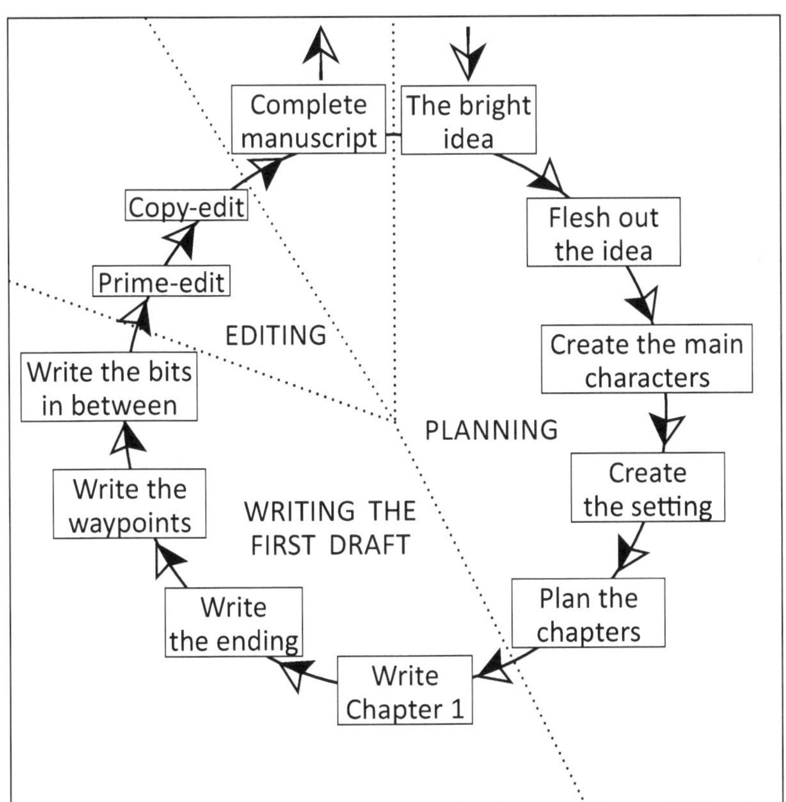

The diagram is shown as a circle because the starting point — the book you aim to write — should match the end point which is your completed novel. Take a moment to think about that. Then consider the age-old maxim: if you don't know where you are going, you will never know when you get there. Using this method, you will know exactly what sort of book you want to write, and you will know where you are going at each stage of the book's development.

Note that I call the starting point a bright idea. This is the firm foundation upon which you will build your story. Without that foundation, your novel will stand upon shaky ground. From that starting point, you will flesh out the bright idea, create the plot, the main characters and the setting, and finally you will plan your chapters. These elements make up the planning stage of the novel-writing process.

When you come to the writing stage of the process, you will write the first chapter and then you will write the ending. The ending is your destination and I will show you exactly how you can plan it in advance. After this you will write 'waypoint' chapters which will help you keep track of your story as you go along. The name of my method comes from the importance that I place on getting the waypoints written before you write the bits in between. For me the waypoints are the guiding lights that help me keep going and also keep me on track towards my planned destination.

Once you have the first draft written, you're by no means done. There's still a lot of work to do to get your novel into shape. Prime-editing and copy-editing are absolutely essential in making a book of high quality.

After the meticulous editing, your novel will be finished — and you'll be ready to send it out to the world!

Although I have briefly outlined the Waypoint Method

here, there is a lot more to explain. I suggest you read this book from cover to cover first. Of course, no one is stopping you from skipping straight to the bits that interest you most, but if you're a first-time novelist, you're bound to get more out of this book if you adopt a more systematic approach.

There is one important point I want you to grasp right from the start: *if you plan your novel carefully, you can write a publishable novel without resorting to tears.* I have used everything that follows in order to plan and create my stories. Now I offer you the chance to benefit from what I have learned, and to take your story onto the road to publication.

So, let's get started.

STAGE 1
PLANNING

STAGE 1
PLANNING

In this part of the book we will look at the planning stage of the writing process, namely, coming up with a basic idea, fleshing out this idea, creating the plot, characters and setting, and finally putting it all together and planning the chapter structure.

However, before we get into the detail, let's look at what makes a good commercial story. This will be useful in knowing what we're aiming at.

The elements of a story

All good novels are based around a story. Of course they are, I hear you say, because fiction is all about stories. But what is a story? You really ought to know what a story is before you start to write one. So let's be clear, right now, what we mean by a story in the context of commercial fiction.

We can easily recognise the moment when we come across a good story. After reading it, we will put down the book and say to ourselves (or others), "That was a really good story. I enjoyed reading it." We may even be clear in our minds what makes it good. We will instinctively register what makes enjoyable reading: the emotion, the characterisation, or the descriptive powers. But do we ever stop to analyse what makes it a story? It may be a romance, a crime novel or an adventure tale. It doesn't matter what the genre is, there is always a basic structure that makes it a story. If you know what that structure is, you are well placed to construct your own story.

So, let's look a bit deeper into what we mean by a story.

I always begin any new novel-writing task by asking myself these four questions:

1. *Who is the main character in this story?*
2. *What is that character's problem?*
3. *What's preventing a simple solution?*
4. *How does it all pan out in the end?*

I want you to read those lines again because this is at the heart of all good novel writing. This is important. You want to write a story, but you will not succeed unless you know what a story is.

At its heart, a story has four elements:

1. *A main character (or characters)*
2. *A problem for the character(s) to solve*
3. *Something preventing a solution*
4. *A dénouement or ending*

Gather together those four elements in a cohesive form and you have a story. I can't emphasise that too much. Analyse any successful novel and you will always find those four elements because that is what a story is all about. So, doesn't it make sense to ensure you have all the elements in place before you start to write the story? Isn't it logical to ask yourself those four questions right at the start?

Of course it is.

And therein lies another good reason for planning your novel.

So, what is a story?

I have read various definitions in different books. None of them totally satisfied my understanding of what we mean by a story within the context of commercial fiction. So I have constructed a definition that is meaningful to me, one that encapsulates all the essential elements in this context.

> *A story is an account of an incident, or series of incidents, set around a defined character or characters, beset with a problem or problems, which they have difficulty resolving. The story will encompass some resolution to the problem(s).*

I suggest you keep that definition in mind as you read on.

In my initial planning, I always ask myself the four key questions. When I can answer them in simple sentences, I know I am ready to create a structure for a new novel. A new story. When I have that structure, I know the whole thing is going to work even though I haven't written one word of the manuscript. At that stage, I have the scaffolding upon which I can build the bricks and mortar of my story.

We'll come back to these four questions later.

The importance of having a bright idea for your story

All good novels are based around a basic concept. It can be a universal truth, a moral or a message the writer wants to pass on to the world at large. The way in which that concept is put across — the foundation upon which the plot is built — is something I think of as a 'bright idea'.

John Bunyan had a religious moral he wanted to put across to the world. He wrapped it up in a 'bright idea' about a pilgrim's journey from 'this world' to 'the world to come'. The result was *Pilgrim's Progress*. It's a story that has passed the test of time.

Closer to our present time, Nevil Shute wanted to pay tribute to a Dutch lady who was caught up in the World War II Japanese occupation of Sumatra. He wrapped it up in a 'bright idea' story of a group of women forced to trek from place to place because no one wanted responsibility for them. He called it *A Town Like Alice*. You may have seen the film.

Coming almost up to date, Edward Lanyon (also published by my publisher, Cloudberry) disliked the inaccuracies of the *Braveheart* film and wanted to show the world the other side of the story. He wanted to create a more accurate account of the Anglo-Scottish wars. That was his starting point, his 'bright idea'. He wrapped up the concept in a tale of an aging English knight caught up in the conflict, and he called it *The Poisoned Cup*.

Before you write your novel, stop and take time to sort out the concept you want to write about and the bright idea you are going to use to put the concept across. If you are not clear about what you want to say to the world, you will have no foundation upon which to build your plot. So get that bright idea fixed in your mind. Don't even sit at your computer until you are quite clear about that germ of creation. That's so easy to say and, for a beginner, so difficult to accept. I can almost hear the potential novelist begging for an easier, quicker way of getting stuck into the actual writing process.

Sorry, I don't know of one that has any real chance of success.

I'll repeat the message because I want you to get the principle firmly in your mind: *your novel should be based upon a concept and created around a bright idea.* If you haven't got that idea, don't start writing. It's unlikely to work.

I have, many times, heard new writers told, "Just sit at your computer and write anything that comes into your mind. The story ideas will come to you eventually." That's great if usable story ideas do come to you easily, but too often they don't and the new writer ends up in a mental cul-de-sac, not sure how to get out of it. Some will slink away and never again bother trying to write a story. The disheartening effect is profound. I have seen it happen. I have spoken to people who have been caught in this trap and often they are ashamed to openly admit their failure. Has it happened to you? Have you sat at your computer, staring at a blank screen because no ideas come to the fore? Or have you started writing and, after a few thousand words, met a brick wall? The plot seems to be going nowhere. Maybe you've written twenty thousand words and you are waiting for the next plot twist to spring into your mind, but nothing comes. Your mind is blank. Have you had to reluctantly concede that your novel is not going to work? What a waste of time and effort. And how disheartening.

I never sit at my computer and hope for ideas to flow spontaneously because experience has told me that I will never achieve a successful novel that way. The very fact of sitting at my computer, willing myself to come up with new ideas, can put unnecessary stress upon my thinking process. It can create a mental block which will have a detrimental effect. My advice to you is clear: don't do it. Don't sit in front of a blank screen hoping and praying for inspiration. Your concentration may be the very thing preventing you from finding that bright spark which will be the seed of your new novel.

If I want new ideas to grow inside my head, I need to relax. I need to feel I am under no pressure. I always keep my mind open for new ideas, but I don't *force* them to appear. I'll explain that in more detail later.

You'll have to experiment and discover what helps you relax. I find my most productive thinking time is early in the morning, before I get dressed. If I'm awake early and my wife is still asleep, I lie in bed quietly, allowing my mind to freely wander around my next story. I may be thinking up new ideas or I may be pondering over developmental ideas. Invariably, answers just pop into my head as I lie there, simply because I am under absolutely no pressure. When I'm ready, I get up, make myself a cup of tea, and then jot down those ideas in a pocket notebook while they are still fresh in my mind. They are, at this point, jotted down only as incomplete ideas, not as fully-formed sentences.

I live in a beautiful part of Dorset and each week I spend one day walking in the countryside with a group of friends. We usually ramble off the beaten track in places that are incredibly peaceful. That is where I often get inspired. As I stroll along, under no stress or anxiety, my mind wanders without any conscious effort and I spontaneously come up with more basic ideas for my stories. It reinforces that important point: the best ideas come when I am not under pressure.

Of course those ideas have to be sparked off by something. Probably the most frequent question I am asked by my readers is, "How do you spark off the ideas for your books?" I tell them about my need to be in a relaxed frame of mind, and then I say to them, "Of course, the sources for my ideas are there right now, all around, just waiting to be kicked into life."

"Really?" they reply, as if it's a revelation to them.

For me, finding a source of ideas is not the most difficult part of writing a novel. It should be the same for you. All you need to do is open your mind to what you see around you. The ideas are there in your newspapers, in the books you read, in the experiences of your friends and neighbours. They are there in your own life experiences. The source of ideas is boundless. All that is needed from you is recognition. When you watch the evening television news broadcast, do you ever find a real news story sparking off an idea for a new work of fiction? When your friends tell you of a strange experience, does it not give you an idea that could make an interesting novel? When you read a published novel, do you never think to yourself how you would have tackled that plot in a totally different way?

Ideas abound for any sort of book. However, there is one big pitfall you should avoid: *don't* write what someone else has suggested to you unless it is something you are genuinely interested in.

If you go to a writers' conference, you will almost certainly hear an agent or publisher say that they are looking for manuscripts within one or two particular genres. It may come out as something like, "We want more historical novels because they are doing well at the moment." Fine, but if you run straight home and look for a new idea within the historical genre, you may come up against two major problems. The first is that a year from now, when your manuscript is complete, historical novels will probably be on the back burner, yet again. Fiction publishing goes like that. The second problem is that you may not be particularly interested in historical novels. You may have chosen to write one simply to fill the gap the agent or publisher has opened up. Believe me, if that is true, it will show in your writing.

My advice is that you should look for new ideas only within the genre that genuinely interests you. If romantic novels are your main interest, stick to writing romantic fiction and not sci-fi thrillers. Writing what the agent wants in the belief that it will be sure to get you published is a major tactical mistake. People who go down that path often try to copy the work of other writers, but they miss out on what made that other writer's work fresh and appealing. The other writer loved the genre, wallowed in it, and it showed in the quality of writing. That was why his/her books were published. If you don't love the genre, your writing may appear stilted and dull.

Okay, you've got a favourite genre and you're looking for a new story idea within that genre. You've got your computer switched off (good) and you're relaxed enough to allow ideas to flow through your mind. Some people find that this is enough and the new ideas start appearing as if by magic. But what if you are struggling and can't seem to come up with anything usable? There's no need to despair as there are ways in which you can prompt ideas, ways in which you can tickle your brain cells into sending the right images into your conscious mind.

Cast your thoughts back through your own life and linger over any strange occurrences that have affected you. Is there an idea there, waiting to surface? What about your relatives and friends? Has anything extraordinary occurred to any of them that might be the spark of inspiration you need? You won't tell that story as it actually happened because the person concerned might be so upset as to take you to court, but you could use it as the basis of an idea.

What about your work environment? Did anything really interesting happen which you could work on and develop into a story? It's an unusual company or organisation which doesn't have a few odd occurrences within its walls. Once again, you'll have to be careful not to libel any of your friends or colleagues.

Still looking for that single bright spark? Here are some of the ways in which I've picked up new ideas:

1. *Responding to someone else's thoughts or comments*
2. *Responding to someone's personal anecdote*
3. *Being inspired by non-fiction books*
4. *Latching on to the subject of a lesson or an interesting learning point*
5. *A story set around a proverb, saying or maxim*
6. *Taking an alternative viewpoint to an existing story*
7. *Researching local or national history*
8. *What did your favourite author(s) write?*

In Appendix A, I will give you some practical examples of each of those techniques. If they give you inspiration, you can freely use them to your heart's content. You can use my own basic ideas in order to kick-start your novel, but please don't steal my book and call it your own.

There is one other point we must consider. That bright spark of an idea is what your novel is going to be all about. When you start writing and get to the last word on the last page, you will need to ask yourself one important question: is this what I intended to write about? Did I stick to that bright spark, or did I wander off track into a wilderness? You'll never know the answer unless you clearly define that basic idea right at the beginning and write it down somewhere.

There is a common saying that writing a novel is one per cent inspiration and ninety-nine per cent perspiration. So far I have talked only about the one per cent: that tiny spark of inspiration. The ninety-nine per cent is yet to come.

How to research your idea

Once you have identified your bright idea, you will need to research it. Never tell yourself, "No one will notice if bits of it are wrong."

Someone will notice.

I was two chapters into reading a thriller by a famous, multi-millionaire author when I came across a really stupid mistake. He described passengers disembarking from an aircraft on the runway at London's Heathrow Airport. Silly boy! Passengers do not disembark on a runway because that would prevent other aircraft from landing or taking off. They disembark on the apron — that's the aircraft parking area adjacent to the terminal building. He can laugh off mistakes like that because he's rich and famous. You can't. You must get things right by starting your research now and continuing with it throughout the writing process. Even if you think you know the subject, you should take time to check your facts. I was recently asked to critique the opening of a novel in which a pilot used the term, "Over and out," when speaking to air traffic control. You may have heard the expression in a cheap movie, but it's wrong. To a pilot and a controller, the words 'over' and 'out' mean contradictory things and are never used together. The message here is something I can't emphasise too much: if you are planning on writing about a story which involves technical matters, you should double-check everything.

You can do your research in various ways, such as:

Surfing the internet

Visiting your local library and, if relevant, specialist libraries

Visiting relevant museums and/or archives (this may be useful if you want to write historical fiction)

Talking to people 'in the know'

My advice is to combine at least two of the above and not to be lulled into a sense of security because just one avenue seems to have given you a quick and easy answer. Double-check anything you are not sure about. Double-check even if you do feel confident about the answer. There are many errors out there, especially if you only rely on the internet as your main source of information.

How to flesh out the idea into a workable plot

'Fleshing out' simply means you are going to give more thought to your basic idea. In other words, you are going to add some meat to the bones. At the moment you have just the germ of an idea, which is great, but you are not yet ready to start writing the story. Apart from anything else, you will want to check that the idea will carry a full-length novel.

Most of my planning is done freehand in a notebook because I'm only making rough notes as I go along. None of it will actually appear in the finished novel. And it doesn't matter that my scrawl is legible only to me.

One advantage of using a notebook — it's pocket-sized, by the way — is that I can jot down ideas as they occur to me, anywhere and at any time of the day or night. I can make notes at home or in the middle of the countryside. I leave my notebook beside the bed at night in case an idea is running around inside my head when I wake up. Not only ideas. I will also jot down a few questions which need answering before I start writing. While I use a notebook, you could, of course, make those notes on your iPad or mobile phone — basically anything that is portable and easy to access. If you're looking for suitable software, you could explore:

- *Scrivener (www.literatureandlatte.com/scrivener.php)*
- *Evernote (www.evernote.com)*
- *Trello (www.trello.com)*

Modern technology is constantly opening up new opportunities for the writer.

As an example of how ideas can develop, let me take you back to my first full-length, gritty novel. *The Legacy of Shame* is the story of a girl lost in the Amazon rainforest and growing up in a tribal community. She knows she doesn't belong there and she wants to find out who she really is. The basis of that novel is the girl's search for her roots. That was my bright idea, the one that started the ball rolling. That was what the story was going to be all about. Although I began with that simple plotline, there were many questions I had to ask myself before

I was ready to develop the concept into a chapter-by-chapter format:

How did she get lost in the jungle?

Who were her parents, and what happened to them?

Who was going to help her escape?

Most important of all, what would she find when she eventually reached the outside world?

I thought about this for some time and jotted down some incomplete answers in my notebook. My ideas came quite randomly at this stage, but they gradually evolved into something more cohesive. It was at this stage, also, that I began to wonder *how* I was going to tell the girl's story. Would I tell it entirely from her first person viewpoint, or would I tell it from a third person observer's viewpoint. I wanted to be clear on this right at the start. A mistake here could lead to many thousands of words being scrapped. Eventually, I decided that the story could not be told as a first person narrative because I needed to delve deep into the minds of other characters. It was the girl's story, but the thoughts and actions of other people were going to be crucial.

After a period of further deliberation, I decided to begin the novel with the girl's mother who had, years ago, given up her child for adoption at birth. My decision on where to begin wasn't taken suddenly. It wasn't a spur-of-the-moment choice. It was something I thought about and deliberated over for some considerable time. I decided to use the first few chapters as a way of engineering how the mother would meet the girl for the first time since giving her away. This would, of course, take place sometime after her daughter had escaped from the forest. I would then let the girl tell her mother the story of what had happened in the jungle. That would form the heart of the novel. How was I going to engineer the meeting? A letter out of the blue would be a good start, I decided. The mother would now be married to a man who was not the girl's father and the letter about the girl would be a bombshell in their family. A family bombshell in Chapter 1? Yes, that should capture the readers' attention, I decided. Make them want to read on. It was also an opportunity to build in some high emotion.

Keep in mind that these were only disjointed thoughts at this point. I didn't yet have a full plot outline. I would have to decide later where and how the girl and her mother would meet and what would happen next. Why did I decide to bring in that meeting between mother and daughter early in the book? I settled on that decision because I wanted to describe the horror the girl's mother felt when she learned her daughter's story. I wanted that sense of horror to grab the reader early in the narrative. It was a ploy that would allow me to dredge up every last scrap of human emotion, and I wanted this to be a very emotional story right from the outset.

Having made that decision, I then had to go back to the question of how the girl got into the jungle in the first place. In fact, that wasn't difficult to work out. I'd indulged in a considerable amount of research, including reading books about Amazonian tribes still hiding from the outside world. The story I hit upon had the girl adopted by wildlife explorers. They would take her with them on an expedition to film such a tribe. They would be killed by fierce tribesmen and the child would be captured.

I was getting quite excited when I jotted down these rough ideas into my notebook. It sounded like I was gradually creating something that would work. So, how could the girl escape back to civilisation, and who would help her? At this point I conjured up the idea of a group of nuns who would set up a missionary camp near the tribal village. Why nuns? Well, I wanted the girl to have female companions who would understand her better than any male explorer could. It seemed the best way to develop her emotions and her inner feelings.

All of this came out, bit by bit, and was jotted down into my notebook. I was nowhere near actually writing the story, but I was amassing a whole load of notes that would eventually help me construct a full-length novel. I felt confident at this stage — before I had written a single word of narrative — that the plot would work. That confidence was important to me because I could see that it was going to be a lengthy novel and I had no intention of wasting time with false starts.

While I was thinking through the plot line, I kept harping back to those four questions I mentioned earlier:

1. *Who is the main character in this story?*
2. *What is that character's problem?*
3. *What's preventing a solution?*
4. *How does it all pan out in the end?*

Use those questions wisely and they will help you flesh out your novel. Jot down your answers and don't worry about the grammar you use. Just get some very rough answers down on paper. And then study them. Think about them. Turn them over in your mind. Begin to make sense of them. Begin to structure the answers. Then add weight to your initial answers, develop them, flesh them out.

It is important that you determine your main character

early in the fleshing out process. If you don't, there's a real risk that a secondary character might become more interesting and take over the limelight. It's one of those pitfalls that pantsers have to be aware of.

One of the real problems of writing a novel off the cuff — the pantsers' way of doing it — is that the characters are not even partially developed at the start. What begins as the main character might fade into the background as the story develops. That will alter the whole ethos of the novel. However, that is not going to happen in your manuscript.

The main character in *The Legacy of Shame* is the girl who grew up among an Amazonian tribe. She was a great character and when I fleshed out the basic idea, it became clear that everything had to revolve around her. However, when I came to set out the chapter-by-chapter plan, I decided that she would not appear in Chapter 1 or Chapter 2. Nevertheless, it was her story and she had to be there in the background, so I made sure she was the source of a major family problem... the letter out of the blue. In the opening chapters she was, like Daphne du Maurier's *Rebecca*, the unseen figure who was always at the heart of the story. When we first meet the girl in Chapter 3, we already know something about her. We have more than an inkling of the problems she faces. And we know that we're going to learn a lot more as the story progresses because it's her story. You see what I mean? Even when she's not in the picture, the other characters are thinking about her, talking about her or acting on her behalf. She is the catalyst for everything that happens to the other characters in the book.

It's not just the beginning of your novel that needs fleshing out. You should also be thinking ahead to the ending. If you know — before you start writing— how the novel will end, you are unlikely to get lost along the way.

The worst sort of novel has an ending that's illogical and unreal. It leaves you wondering, "So what?" or "I don't believe it!" And it tells you the author hadn't thought — right at the start — how the story would end. In all probability, the writer couldn't find a satisfying solution on reaching the last page. Don't get yourself caught up in that trap. Decide now, before you start on the manuscript, how your story will end in a logical and satisfying way. Then you will be able to develop the plot in a consistent manner between the beginning and the end.

The ending should be logical, but not obvious. And that applies also to the way you flesh out various 'conflict' or 'problem' incidents that make up each chapter. For example, in my novel, *The Legacy of Secrets*, I needed to kill off a young wartime WAAF (Women's Auxiliary Air Force) called Peggy Higgins. Logic told me it should happen in the London Blitz. But not in an obvious move.

When the raid begins, Peggy and her mum are hiding in a cellar. Both are frightened as I build up the tension. Bombs land nearby and the tension increases. The house next door takes a direct hit. More tension. The house above Peggy and her mum begins to crumble. More tension. Can Peggy survive the raid? The reader wonders what will happen next. Then... yes, Peggy can survive. The next morning, she and her mum crawl out from under the rubble. The tension eases. Peggy meets her dad, an ARP (Air Raid Precautions) warden. He has survived the night. The tension eases further. Peggy is told to go to her aunt's house and make a cup of tea. Relief all round. But I am playing games with the reader. As Peggy enters her aunt's house, she triggers an unexploded bomb...! I got the outcome I wanted, but I engineered it in a way that wasn't obvious. And all of this was part of my planning.

I suspect that had I not thought it out beforehand, I might have ended up with a chapter in which the tension rose and rose without waver until Peggy died in the cellar. Teasing the reader in the way I did was something that had to be thought out in advance, something that had to be planned for maximum effect.

Now turn the lesson from that incident into the strategy for the whole book. Thinking out the plot problems (and conflicts) in advance — and knowing how it will end — enables you to make the story twist and turn in ways that are unexpected for the reader (but not for you), ways that could so easily be missed if you were to write with no clear plan in mind.

As you develop a clearer picture of your novel's structure, you can start thinking about subplots and making notes on them. The most important thing to remember about subplots is that they are not separate stories. They are an integral part of the whole book and they must link in with the main plot.

Here are some hypothetical examples of main plots and subplots:

Example 1:

Main plot:

Mr A is a detective inspector who is searching for a serial killer. The killer taunts him with messages about what he will do to Mr A's estranged wife unless he backs off the case. Mr A knows he will have to find the killer soon.

Subplot:

Detective Inspector A is a recovering alcoholic. He has lost his wife and family as a result of his alcoholic past. His continuing struggle to stay off the booze is the subplot.

Example 2:

Main plot:

Miss B is a young office clerk. She is in love with a man who is married and will not leave his wife. The main plot centres around Miss B's discovery that the wife is also having an affair. Should she tell her lover or not? Miss B and her lover's wife end up helping one another.

Subplot:

Miss B has a fixation about her weight. She hires a personal trainer to help her get slim. She thinks this will make her lover like her more, but the trainer takes a fancy to her. This is a subplot which could give you an excuse for lots of twists and turns as well as some humour.

In both examples, the subplot adds something to the main plot and also adds some dimension to the main character(s). You should be thinking about your subplots now, not after you start writing the manuscript. If you find they are taking on a life of their own and straying from the main plot, stop here. Better to curtail the subplots now than when you have many thousands of words committed to your computer.

How long you spend on the fleshing-out process will depend upon your story and how complex it will become. I suggest you don't rush things. You can carry your notebook around with you for a few weeks, jotting down the ideas as they come to you. Keep in mind that writing a novel may well take the best part of a year, maybe more, so a few weeks fleshing out the idea will be only a small part of the total exercise.

You can stop to think at any time and ask yourself: *What would happen if...? Suppose this happens, what then...?* And jot down a few answers. They don't have to be coherent at this stage, nor might you actually use those ideas in the completed story. They're just random thoughts to start with, but a fuller picture will slowly emerge. Don't force it; allow it to happen at its own rate. The important thing is to get those notes saved somewhere.

The importance of conflict

Remember the four questions that make up the story?

1. *Who is the main character in this story?*
2. *What is that character's problem?*
3. *What's preventing a solution?*
4. *How does it all pan out in the end?*

Let's turn to the second question (I'll return to the first question later): *What is the main character's problem?* There must be a problem or some form of conflict in your story and, at this stage of your thinking, you should be working out how your main character's problem will fit into your story development.

This is important. A manuscript without problems or conflict is not a novel. It's not even a story. It's a series of bland events. You must get that clear in your head right now. Can you imagine watching an episode of *Coronation Street* or *The Young and the Restless* in which the characters do nothing but chat casually and admire the scenery? It would be absolutely boring. If you do not create conflict between the characters, you will not have a viable story. More importantly, the problem(s) must be central to the theme of the novel, not sideline events. The problem in *Jaws* was the shark attacks, and those attacks were central to the story. The problem for Elizabeth Bennet was Mr Darcy's pride and her prejudice. Pride and prejudice were the source of the central conflict that kept them apart. Everything else was a subplot.

There must be no simple solution to those problems. If you have a quick and simple solution in Chapter 1, what are you going to do with the rest of the novel?

In my novel, *Prestwick,* the main problem was a collision between two aircraft over the North Atlantic. The simple solution would have been to allow both aircraft to land as soon as possible at the nearest airport. End of story. But I had to keep the aircraft airborne through the rest of the book. I had to keep the tension going and the pages turning by constantly making the problem even worse. Just when the pilots thought they were going to reach land, I had the controllers at Prestwick refuse them landing permission. And then, as if things weren't bad enough, I had someone on the ground deliberately interfere with the radio navigation equipment. How were the pilots ever going to find a way out of this?

That story is a thriller, but the idea of conflict is just as important in a romance or a comedy. Where would the stories of Bridget Jones have ended up if she hadn't met with relationship problems? Who would bother to read Sophie Kinsella's shopaholic books if the main character was not hopelessly addicted to shopping? Della Galton's *Ice and a Slice* is another classic example of an addiction problem, featuring a woman with a drinking habit that is dragging her down.

In none of these examples is the solution simply or easily solved. The problem in your novel will last right up to the end of the book. And you now need to work out what the ending will be. You don't want to get six months down the line and then discover there is no real answer to the main problem. Neither do you want to get to the end of the manuscript and discover the only possible solution doesn't fit with the way your characters behave. You need to know now how the book will end so that you can steer the characters along a path that will logically lead to that predetermined, satisfying conclusion... and not some other ending.

The 'don't know' effect

The one thing most likely to grab your readers' attention is an enigma or mystery. Put your readers into a 'don't know' situation and you have a good chance of holding their attention. That doesn't mean you have to write a whodunit to get your novel widely read. It means you have to create questions in the readers' minds. Make sure there is something they don't know and then tease them with it. For example:

Will the girl get her man? (romance)

Will the hero soldier survive the coming battle? (military)

Will the spaceship get back to Earth? (science fiction)

Will the boy wizard meet his nemesis? (young adult/ children's novel)

Sometimes the readers can be quite sure about the answer to those questions before the end of the novel. Maybe it's spelt out in Chapter 1 or, more likely, it's the answer everyone expects. For example, will the girl get her man? Of course she will. That's the obvious dénouement for that sort of romantic novel. Will Richard Sharpe survive the Battle of Talavera? Of course he will — otherwise the following novels in the Sharpe series will be pointless.

So what you have to do now is to change the question:

How will the girl get her man? (romance)

How will the hero soldier survive the coming battle? (military)

How will the spaceship get back to Earth? (science fiction)

How will the boy wizard meet his nemesis? (young adult/children's novel)

It doesn't matter what genre you tackle, you should aim to create a story in which the readers are left wondering about the outcome. They have to read on in order to find out what happens. Sometimes, the key character will also be in a 'don't know' situation, especially in crime novels. Just occasionally, however, the key character will have the answer, but will not divulge it to the reader. The character may even be what is known as an 'unreliable narrator', deliberately lying to the reader. That's a real tease. It's the nature of many a short story with a twist ending, but it can also be used to good effect in a novel.

Character-based stories and plot-based stories

In literary circles there is a lot of discussion about character-based stories and plot-based stories. What's the difference? And does it matter anyway because a good novel must have both plot development and character development. A novel without an underlying plot to keep the reader interested is not a good novel. A novel without characters that grow and develop throughout the story is not a good novel. You need both.

The whole point of the argument about character-based and plot-based stories lies with the balance between the development of the characters and the development of the plot. In Jane Austin's novels, the balance tends towards the characters and the way they grow and change as the stories unfold. The plots exist, but they are subservient to the characters. The plots are there primarily to carry the characters, bring them into sharp relief, and allow them to develop.

In contrast, Colin Dexter's crime novels shift the balance towards the plot. The main characters — Morse and Lewis — exist and are well drawn, but they are there primarily to shift the plot forward. We keep reading the books because we want to know who killed the victims and why. That doesn't mean Inspector Morse is a two-dimensional character, far from it, but his purpose is to lead us along the road of discovery.

Your novel may be a character-based story — in other words, the balance will lead the reader towards a deeper empathy with the lead character — or it may be a plot-based novel. In the latter case its success will be dependent upon the reader becoming engrossed in how the key character tackles the action. But don't be misled by the distinction. Both types of novels will depend upon you bringing your characters to life, and this is the moment to start thinking about them in some depth. Flesh out your characters now. Give them some telling characteristics so that they will behave appropriately when you fit them into the plot. For example, Morse's purpose is to carry the action forward, but he is also a rounded character in his own right.

So, it will be your task to animate your characters, develop them and make them grow into believable people your readers will care about. If your readers don't care what happens to your creations, the book will fail. What makes a page-turner work is not that the reader wants to know what happens next, it's that the reader wants to know what happens *to your characters.*

Protagonists and antagonists

Most readers will think of the protagonists as the goodies and the antagonists as the baddies, but that's not actually correct. The protagonist is the main character in a novel and he/she can be good or bad. The main character in *A Christmas Carol* was Ebenezer Scrooge, so he was the protagonist. But he was certainly not a goodie. The main character in *Pride and Prejudice* was Elizabeth Bennet, so she was the protagonist and she had quite a different nature to Scrooge.

In any commercial novel, the protagonist will:

a) always have a problem to solve
b) always undergo some form of change as the story progresses

Scrooge had a major problem: his miserly behaviour. That behaviour had to change as the novel progressed. The Scrooge in the final chapter was quite unlike the Scrooge at the opening of the story. Elizabeth Bennet's problem was the behaviour of Mr Darcy. In the early stages of the book, she disliked him, but her attitude changed as the book progressed.

The antagonist is the person who stands against the main character. Whatever the main character does or wants, the antagonist will oppose it. The antagonist will:

a) always work against the protagonist's intent
b) never change

Scrooge had three antagonists working against him. They were the Ghosts of Christmas Past, Present and Yet to Come. They stood against his bad nature and they were the ones who succeeded in making Scrooge change. Elizabeth Bennet's main antagonist was Mr Darcy. It can be argued that he did little or nothing to change his own behaviour as the story progressed. It was Elizabeth — the protagonist — who changed her opinion and attitude.

Keep these points in mind when you are populating your story.

How to create interesting characters

Let's begin this section with another bit of myth-busting. The pantsers — so it's said — find it easier to bring their characters to life because they have a blank canvas to work on. Not true, I suggest. The basic techniques of bringing a character to life apply equally to whichever technique you use to write your story. The only difference is that the planners know — right from the start — exactly what sort of characters they need to create in order for the plot to work. The pantsers don't. They make it up as they go along, and they may well have to go back and change their characters later as the plot begins to evolve. If they devise a character before they know the plot, they may well discover they are hemmed in with what that character can or cannot do. Their options may become limited.

So, what do you need to think about when you design your

characters (regardless of whether they are heroes/heroines, villains or somewhere in between)?

Let's begin with their names. Those names matter because we automatically make subconscious judgements about people, dependent upon their names. In everyday life our names are important to the public image we create. That's why Lord Stansgate, a Labour politician in the UK, changed his name from Anthony Wedgewood Benn to plain Tony Benn. Arthur Scargill might never have become a miners' leader had he been called Cuthbert Willoughby-Smythe. Would Marion Morrison have become famous as a hard-living cowboy if he hadn't changed his name to John Wayne?

Let's imagine that you are in the shoes of Barbara Cartland and you plan a novel about a debutante living in the 1920s. Would you call her Ethel Utterthwaite? Probably not. It doesn't create the right public image. But suppose you were in the shoes of Catherine Cookson, writing about a girl living in poverty in a Northern English mill town. Her parents are dead and she has been brought up by her aunt, Ethel Utterthwaite. That would work. The point is that the name must fit the image you want that character to put across.

When you choose the names, pay attention to three factors: the character's age, social background and the period of the story. It's not an easy matter because you can run the risk of stereotyping your character simply by choice of name, and we all know that stereotyping is something to be avoided. So, make it a balance. Choose a name that adds character, but stays within clearly defined limits. Don't call your Edwardian debutante Ethel Utterthwaite, and don't call her Hortensia Harcourt-Pemberton-Moneyworthy (unless your humorous plot line makes it essential). Don't call your trade union leader Cuthert Willoughby-Smythe and don't call him Bert Boggins.

If you do, don't expect your publisher to be happy about it. There are exceptions to every rule, of course. What are we to make of the name Endeavour Morse? It probably goes outside those defined limits, but it works because it governs the character's behaviour throughout the series.

Think long and hard about a choice of name that will help in the process of creating character. And think real life. Catherine Middleton: what a perfect name for a beautiful commoner destined to become queen.

Just as we shouldn't go overboard in stereotyping characters by their names, so it's important not to stereotype characters by the way they look, in other words, the way you describe them. In my novel, *The Legacy of Secrets*, I created a feisty young woman who carries much of the plot. But I didn't want to create the sort of stereotypical perfect woman who appears in so many Hollywood movies. So, in my book, her face is physically damaged. It was my way of giving a new physical angle to a heroic character. It also affected the way she behaved.

Bear in mind that characters which were new and interesting when they first appeared in print — James Bond, for instance — will come across as clichéd stereotypes if you try to recreate them today. Send any publisher a story about a handsome alpha male secret agent with all the good looks any girl would swoon for and you'll have a hard time selling it. It's been done too many times before.

How you describe a character's appearance will be important. Try not to resort to the tired old descriptions such as: she had clear blue eyes, or he was tall and handsome. You can jot such descriptions into your notebook if you can't think of anything better, but when you come to the manuscript, you will want something that conjures up a fresh image in the reader's mind. If you are able to formulate more precise and evocative descriptions now, you will be well placed later.

Think of sentences such as:

She looked frail as a china figurine, so easily damaged.

Her hair was like ebony lacquer, newly applied and gleaming in the sunlight.

His face was a relief map, contoured by a lifetime of troubles.

His tired old frame was stooped until it seemed almost beyond the point of balance.

As you think of these descriptions, jot them down. They will be invaluable when you come to write the manuscript.

In addition to how your characters look, think about their personality and background in a wider sense. For example, to create a rounded character, you could think about these aspects:

Name

Age

Physical characteristics

Family background

Behaviour

Personality

Occupation

Interests and hobbies

Values and motivations

Fears and worries

Character flaws

As well as the detailed notes, you will need a quick précis: a description of each main character which will be useful when you start work on the manuscript. Don't make this description too long. The shorter it is, the easier it will be to refer to. I mentioned a feisty young woman in my novel, *The Legacy of Secrets*. This is how I described her in my notes:

Name: Katherine Penrice

Age: Twentyish

Appearance: Great figure, but a mangled face

Behaviour: Forthright. Not afraid to say what she thinks

Personality: Breezy. No sense of introspection

Failing: Too quick to put herself forward

And this is what I wrote about her boyfriend:

Name: Colin Portesham

Age: Late twenties

Appearance: Alpha male with glasses (a bit Clark Kentish)

Behaviour: Very caring, too much so maybe.

Personality: Too serious. Doesn't know when to have a laugh

Failing: A bit slow to take full control of his own life

When I came to write that particular manuscript, I further developed each character both in appearance and personality, but I was always building upon those basic notes. That was when Katherine Penrice was given long blonde hair and her strength of character grew to become an overriding factor in the story.

Take time to think about your characters because you will want them to fit in with the plot, and you won't want them to act in a way that goes against their personalities. If you design them well, they will carry the plot nicely. If you design them badly, they may end up doing things that go against the story-line... or behaving out of character.

Here's another useful bit of advice: never think of your main character as yourself. It's not you; it's someone you created, someone who doesn't even exist, except inside your head. Your character may not behave in the way you would behave under certain pressures. Ian Fleming was not James Bond and Helen Fielding was not Bridget Jones. You are not the star of your masterpiece, so don't make that character do what you would do when the chips are down. Make each of your characters do what they would choose to do as *their* story unfolds.

Character flaws and character development

I've attended many writers' conferences, seminars and summer schools and I've heard most of the common advice given to new writers. Some of it is helpful; some is actually confusing. Take this bit of well-intentioned guidance: *make your main character sympathetic.* What does that mean? Is James Bond a *sympathetic* character? Does 'sympathetic' mean the main character should, for example, be eminently likeable? Maybe, maybe not. Unless we add some extra detail, the would-be novelist could be led astray by that advice.

I prefer to tell new writers: make your main character *flawed*. After all, that is the very nature of the human being. James Bond is certainly flawed, and Fleming was right to make him so. We come into this life in order that we should learn from our experiences because we are all flawed in some way. So, let's make our fictional characters imperfect. Let's give them a reason for their lives on earth. Let's make them behave like real human beings, not cardboard cut-outs.

Sophie Kinsella's shopaholic is flawed in her shopping habit, and that's what makes readers warm to her. She is human like the rest of us. Bernard Cornwell's Sharpe is flawed in his need for recognition and that's what gets him into exciting scrapes. Inspector Morse is flawed in his drinking habit and it ultimately kills him. But it makes him a very interesting character. Like him or not, you cannot ignore him.

The main reason for making your key character flawed lies in the opportunities it gives for his or her personal development. It allows opportunities for the character to change as the story progresses. In other words, the character must somehow be different at the end of the novel. He or she may not fully overcome the flaw, but should at least have gone some way to recognising it. Morse knew his problem. He never overcame it, but he recognised it in the latter days when he sat at home, too ill to be at work. So, here's an element of your story which you need to think about now. What will your main character be like at the start of the story, and what will he or she be like at the end? The change could be the main theme in your plot, or it could be a subplot. Either way, you need to work on it now.

At the start of my *Prestwick* novel — the one where two aircraft collide — First Officer Dougie Nyle is unable to face the implications of the loss of a child. One of the effects of the airborne catastrophe in which he finds himself throughout the story is to make him face up to reality. He must determine the sort of future he wants for himself and his wife. By the end of the book, his inability to face up to his loss — his flaw — is overcome.

Harry Potter's main flaw is his meekness and uncertainty, but here's the clever bit: that meekness is a factor of the way he has been treated by his devious aunt and uncle. By taking him away to Hogwarts School of Witchcraft and Wizardry, J.K. Rowling gives him the opportunity to allow his underlying bravery to develop. At the end of the Harry Potter series, the main character has changed enormously. His flaws are firmly behind him.

That last example is important because it underlines the premise that the character must be *capable* of overcoming the flaws. There is no point in starting out with a weak character who simply doesn't have the ability to become a brave hero. That character is not going to change. You might contrive to make such a character act bravely, but it won't be convincing. Devise a flaw that can be realistically overcome, or at least recognised.

The world your characters inhabit

We all inhabit the same world, don't we? Well, yes, in some respects. We all live on the same planet Earth, even if that world has many physically different regions. But, when you come to write a novel, there is more to consider than just the physical world.

Harry Potter's life was constrained by far more than the walls of Hogwarts School. He was constrained by his personal background — the loss of his parents, the cruelty of his aunt and uncle, the looming threat of Voldemort. He was also constrained by the behaviour of his friends and enemies, by the structure of authority within the school and the rules of the wider wizarding world. That was his world and everything in his story had to reflect his personal background and his relationships.

Consider, also, the differences you must take into account if your story is set in another era. The 'world' of the Tudor dynasty bore little resemblance to the 'world' of today. Everyday life in Tudor times and — most importantly — common attitudes were quite different from those we encounter today. This is an important point which you must think about before you begin to write. Right from the start, your Tudor characters must be set in *their* world, not our own modern-day world. You cannot have the words, "Okay. Right on, old sport. We'll give it a go," tumbling from the lips of King Henry. In his world, those expressions did not exist. In Henry's world, the king's first duty was to defend his realm, by whatever means were considered necessary. His daughter, Elizabeth, never took up physical arms like her father, but her whole life was geared towards defending her realm... her 'world'... even if it meant ordering the lopping off of a head or two.

No modern English monarch would countenance such an act because our world is radically different. We live in a world with different ideas, different concepts and different standards of behaviour. That is something would-be novelists sometimes forget, and even some readers frequently forget when they criticise the behaviour of historical characters.

In my opinion, the most common errors with historical novels lie with those told in first person. Those are the novels where the author gets the historical facts right, but the style of narration is clearly set in the modern world. The author is the 'I' character living within that past age, so the author should pay some heed to the way stories were once told. That doesn't mean writing the novel totally in the style of, say, John Bunyan, but rather it means avoiding any comments that clearly say, "I am a twenty-first century writer with a twenty-first century way of thinking."

Even when writing a story set in the modern world, we must be careful in creating the world of the characters. When I wrote *The Legacy of Shame* — set in the present era — I needed to research the lives of primitive tribes in the Amazon rainforest before I started writing about that particular world. The lives of those tribesmen bear little resemblance to anything we might experience in a modern society. Within the tribes, I needed the characters to behave in a way that reflected their own tribal world.

When I wrote *The Legacy of Conflict*, I drew upon my own experiences of life in Northern Ireland at the time of the recent Troubles. The two main characters — sisters parted soon after birth — grew up in very different worlds. One was the product of wealth and comfort in England while the other grew up in relative poverty and violence in the backstreets of Belfast. Those different worlds made their forms of behaviour — their actions, their thoughts, their beliefs — vastly different. It was more than just a matter of right or wrong; it was a case of understanding the worlds in which they grew up.

What world will your main characters inhabit? Depending on where and how your story unfolds, you may have to think about more than just one location. And some novels — such as those in the genres of science fiction, fantasy and historical fiction — require a more detailed world-building process than others. If you're struggling with constructing your setting, you may find it helpful to start by considering the relevant areas from this prompt list:

Name of the place

Time period

Geographical boundaries (and what's beyond those boundaries)

Physical features

Climate

Natural resources

Architecture

History of the place

Transportation and travel

Distinctive sounds, sights and smells of the place

Government system and politics

Social organisation

Crime, punishment and the legal system

Warfare

Technology

Economic activity (e.g. how people make a living, business and industry)

Living standards

Education

Religion and/or belief system

Ethics and values

Customs

Population (e.g. the number of people, ethnic diversity, generational differences)

Family life

Language

Medicine, health and wellbeing

Leisure activities

Food and eating

Fashion and dress

Arts and entertainment

Think about your setting carefully; you need to get it right before you start writing your novel.

Imaginary worlds

Not all writers place their characters into the real world. Writers of science fiction and fantasy novels create environments which do not exist in reality. Most of the detail of life in that world comes directly from the writer's imagination.

J.R.R. Tolkien began by creating a fictitious language. You will probably not want to go down that road. My advice is to begin in exactly the same way you would begin any novel: first come up with a bright idea. You can spark off that idea by asking yourself the question: what do you want to say to the world with this novel?

My one favourite sci-fi novel is *The Chrysalids* by John

Wyndham. He's dead now so I can't ask him what he had in mind when he began writing that book back in the 1950s, but I can speculate, and I can tell you what bright idea shines through to me, the reader. The story is set in a post-apocalyptic future in which humans are forced to learn again lessons in humanity that have been lost from the time before the apocalypse. They are human Chrysalids, in an early stage of social and ethical thinking. They see life in terms of fundamental religious dogmas, a process of thinking in which any deviation from a self-imposed norm must be eradicated. Anyone who isn't like them is an abhorrence and must be eliminated. The story was published in 1955, but the bright idea I take from it is very relevant for today. Wyndham was a writer ahead of his time.

In that novel, Wyndham created a physical world that can be seen in many post-apocalyptic films and books. His real genius was in creating the way people thought and behaved in that world. That is the most important idea I can suggest to anyone writing sci-fi or fantasy: create your physical worlds, yes, but pay far more attention to the way of life within that world. The ethics and values of those characters will best illustrate the message you want to convey within your story.

Sometimes, the writer's imaginary world can be only partially real. For example, my alternative history novel *Bomber Girl* imagines that the German plan to occupy England in 1940 succeeded. It is an imaginary world because it never happened. I created characters who would think and behave in an environment that never existed. Except for the occupation, the physical landscape was real, but the way of behaving was imaginary.

Let me finish this section with one very important message. If you set your novel in the real world of today, you will have little difficulty in maintaining the consistency of the environment and the rules that exist within it. After all, you live in that world and you know how it works. If, however, you set your story in an imaginary world, the environment and the rules of how people think and behave will be alien — to you and to your readers. That is where problems can occur and inconsistencies can creep in. You should avoid introducing any blatant discrepancy into that world, even if you can see no other way of getting the main characters out of a tricky situation. It could be something as simple as suddenly introducing time travel in the last chapter because there is no other way of escaping from an alien environment. The time travel element should have been set as a parameter right at the start. Or, it may be that the main characters change their fundamental way of thinking halfway through the story in order to progress the plot. It is important that you define the rules of your imaginary world right at the start and ensure that your characters stay within them. Your imaginary world must not have rules that change randomly. Even if you dream up the weirdest possible world and have the weirdest possible rules within it, you must make sure everything functions in a way that stays consistent and logical.

How to plan the chapters in line with the plot

By now you may be anxious to get into the nitty-gritty writing process, but you must not rush it. If you miss this next stage, you could end up with real problems in months to come. It's that important. Imagine that you are six months down the line and you have fifty thousand hard-grafted words committed to your computer. Then you meet a plot problem and you can't see any way out of it.

Back to the drawing board.

Or, you see a way out, but it means rewriting the last twenty or thirty thousand words.

Back to the drawing board.

That could be very demotivating, especially if it's your first novel. Better that you sort out all of your structure and plot problems now, before you start on Chapter 1. Keep in mind that old adage:

Failure to prepare is to prepare for failure.

I don't write like a pantser because, to me, it's rather like letting the animals take charge of the zoo. I prefer to be the zookeeper in control of the plot. I let my characters behave only in the way I design them to behave. If a character needs to be bad, I design him to be bad and act badly. If a character needs to be caring, I design him to be caring and act caringly. They never get out of their cages because I design each character to fit the role he or she has to play within the plot.

Another analogy: if your story was a film, you would be in the role of scriptwriter and director. The cast would follow your script in the way you direct them to follow it. You would not allow them to make it all up as they went along, with no idea how it would end. It's the same with a novel. The characters should follow your plan in the way you tell them to follow it. Allow them to express themselves by all means, but make sure they keep to the script. Their feelings and emotion should come through as and when you direct them to come through.

"Doesn't that stifle creativity?" people have asked me. No. In my experience it is quite the opposite. My creative thoughts occur at a time when I can marshal them into a logical order and use them to good effect. They don't get wasted. Because

I know what is going to happen to my characters, I can give a lot of thought to their nature, their characteristics, what makes them tick. I can invent realistic back stories for them. I can give them realistic mannerisms. I can be as creative as I like! Planning doesn't mean that you can't be creative. If I left it all to chance, I would probably have to scrap some good ideas because the plot was being driven in ways I had not anticipated... with an ending I wasn't sure about.

Earlier, I said that your main character must change as the story progresses. That change must be well planned on a chapter-by-chapter basis if it is to work. In my novel, *The Legacy of Conflict*, I created a fascinating female character. Right from the start, I planned that she would appear to have a nasty temperament but would end up as the story's real heroine. It was partly a case of the character changing her behaviour as the story progressed, and partly a case of the reader misjudging her at the start.

Showing a change in her behaviour as the book progressed wasn't easy because it had to be believable. In order to make it convincing, and keep to the story I wanted to tell, I had to enforce a tight rein on the young woman's actions all the way through the book. I allowed her to break into tantrums when the plot demanded it, I allowed her to misbehave atrociously when the plot demanded it, and I allowed her to lower her guard when the time came to reveal the real person behind the mask. Most importantly, *I had to carefully plan the chapters in which the various behaviour changes would occur*. The changes the reader sees in that character had to come about not too soon and not too late. There was no room for reliance upon hope and good luck. Left to chance it would not have worked. Had I written the story as a pantser — making it up on the hoof — the plot would not have worked, and the character would not have come across as believable.

I had to keep to my well-defined chapter-by-chapter structure when I wrote that manuscript, and yet the story is alive with raw emotion. Don't be lured into believing that a tightly-plotted novel will be short on human feelings. Those feelings will exist, but they will come to the surface when the writer's plan dictates, not when the character dictates or — more accurately — when the ideas randomly pop into writer's head while working at the computer.

At some point you will need to gather together all your notes and read through them thoroughly. They should give you an idea of how the story will pan out. Now ask yourself: where will the manuscript begin? It's not always obvious. One of the big mistakes made by new writers is to start a story at the wrong point.

A good technique is known as *get in late — get out early.* 'Get in late' means starting the story where the action begins, and missing out any preliminary fancy descriptions. 'Get out early' means you shouldn't keep writing when the action is over.

Sam Goldwyn, the film producer, would advocate powerful openings to his films. He is reported to have said, "Start with a volcano erupting and then get bigger." You don't have to go to that extreme, but you will need to begin with something important: a hook. It will be something that will capture the reader's attention.

Look at your plot again and ask yourself, "Where does the problem begin?" That's often the right place to start Chapter 1.

Remember that girl lost in the Amazon jungle? I started *The Legacy of Shame* at the point where the husband of the girl's birthmother mistakenly opens a letter from a researcher who is seeking out the girl's real family. That pivotal act turned the whole family into turmoil. The tension started right there in Chapter 1.

At this point you should be ready to sequence your notes into a chapter-by-chapter structure. Take your time over it, making sure you include every aspect of the story that arose in your primary notes. You could turn to an A4 notebook rather than the pocket notebook you've been using. Or you might copy your tablet jottings onto your computer.

The chart on the next page will show you how I began to arrange the opening chapters of my novel *Prestwick*. It is the story of two aircraft which collide over the North Atlantic.

A grid like this is can be a very useful précis of the novel. With this in front of me I know exactly what is going to happen all the way through the book, right up to the last page: I can judge the rhythms of the high points and low points. I can check that the plot works, I can ensure characters are in the right places at the right times, and I can ensure that I haven't missed out any important story developments. And I haven't even begun to write the details of Chapter 1!

Notice how I've annotated the names of the main characters which appear in each chapter. This is to ensure that they each get a fair share of the action and none of them are drowned out by minor characters. I've also annotated the locations so that I have a clear picture of how the action moves logically from place to place.

Don't run away with the idea that I sat at a desk and wrote each analysis in one easy session. It was a developmental process and later pages were marred by items scratched out and rewritten as a better sequence occurred to me. I am constantly open to revision. I have been known to wake up an hour after going to bed and scribble away by the light of a bedside lamp.

Chapter	Action	Characters	Location
1	JFK Airport, New York. Bad weather. Flight ready to depart for Prestwick. First Officer Dougie Nyle is concerned by a police investigation into the death of a stewardess. Suspicious behaviour of Captain MacNabb. Late take-off. Stewardess Maggie Loughlin acting suspiciously. She has to deal with a drunken passenger who has a heart attack.	Dougie Nyle MacNabb Maggie Loughlin	JFK Airport, New York, Aboard 747
2	Flight diverted into Gander to offload sick passenger. Start backstory of MacNabb and dead stewardess. Bring in hint of Loughlin's involvement in the girl's murder.	Nyle MacNabb Loughlin	Gander Airport
	USAF tanker lands at Gander. Crew sent on emergency mission over Atlantic. All dog tired.	Judson	Aboard tanker
	747 departs Gander. MacNabb inputs wrong flight coordinates. Collision seen from 747.	MacNabb	Aboard 747
3	Panic aboard 747. McNabb badly injured. Nyle not on the flight deck. He struggles to get back to his seat.	MacNabb Nyle	Aboard 747
	Panic aboard the tanker. Realisation crew were asleep.	Judson	Aboard tanker

My analysis — let's call it a route map — allows me to judge the novel's rhythm. The manuscript should flow logically and it should have high points and low points. The high points will be the tense parts where the reader will be eager to know what happens next. The low points will be what I think of as 'gathering your breath' moments.

The tension in a well-planned novel will rise throughout the length of the book until the story ends on the highest of the high points — the climax — before the final resolution. But the progress towards the climax should not be a continuous upward curve. If you chart it from start to finish, it might look something like this:

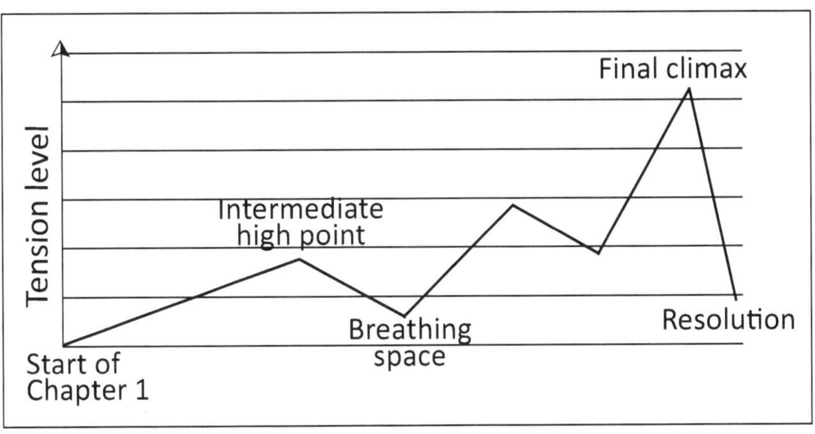

You will not need to construct a similar chart for your novel, but you should have an overall impression in your mind of how the tension ebbs and flows. Think of it as the thumping heart of your story, the heart that beats louder when the tension rises.

There will be certain twists and turns in your story that will rank as absolutely crucial, so important that the whole plot could fall apart if you don't get them right. Some of those twists will stand out anyway, but others might easily get lost or overlooked. So, let's ensure they don't get missed. Read through your analysis — or route map — pick out those important plot lines and underline them.

The three-act structure

In your planning stage, you should give a thought to something known as the three-act structure. This is a way of breaking down a complete story into three component sections. They are:

The set-up

The main conflict

The resolution

The set-up. This will comprise of several of your opening chapters. It may encompass around 15 to 25 per cent of your novel. Think of Harry Potter and the setting-up chapters in the first book in the series. The story does not start at Hogwarts School — the main arena for the complete Potter story — it begins in the Dursley family home. The set-up chapters tell us all we need to know about Harry's background, the problems he has with his adoptive family, and it hints at the major problems to come. The set-up chapters also introduce the other main characters: Dumbledore, Hagrid and the new friends Harry meets on the Hogwarts Express.

The main conflict. This will be the middle section of your novel and will encompass most, if not all of the main conflict areas. Having set up your story to include problems, fights and other forms of struggle, you can now dive into those meaty scenes. This will probably encompass around 60–70% of the entire novel. In the case of Harry Potter, most of these scenes are set in Hogwarts School and involve — in one way or other — Harry's main antagonist, Lord Voldemort.

The resolution. This is the final act which encompasses the dénouement. In the case of a Hercule Poirot story, this is where the great detective gathers together all the suspects and announces his judgement on who did the dirty deed. In an adventure novel, this is where we reach the main climax and the hero or heroine finally escapes from dramatic peril. In a romance novel, this is where the heroine gets her man. In a Western, this is where the good guy guns down the bad guy.

When you have completed the chapter-by-chapter route map, and ensured it complies with all the requirements of a successful story, you will finally be ready to start writing Chapter 1. And here's the important point: you will begin with the sure knowledge that your story is going to work.

It's possible, of course, that your route map will reveal that the story won't work. While you are fleshing out your plot, you may suddenly realise that it is fatally flawed. You may meet a dead end, you may run out of ideas, you may find you don't have a clue where the plot can go next. What do you do?

I'll tell you what. In a word, you should rejoice.

You've discovered that the story in its current form will not work, but you haven't yet started work on the manuscript. You haven't written one single word of that story yet. Imagine how you would feel if you made that discovery after writing thirty or forty thousand words? It's happened. It's happened to too many eager writers who started writing their manuscripts before they had planned the story. Ditching thirty or forty thousand words is soul-destroying. Starting again from scratch, with no clear plan and the risk of making the same mistake is equally demoralising. But that won't happen to you. All you have to lose is a few pages of scribbled notes.

So rejoice.

STAGE 2
WRITING THE FIRST DRAFT

STAGE 2
WRITING THE FIRST DRAFT

Now that you've gone through the planning stage and finished creating the route map for your novel, you can move on to the actual writing process. Using the Waypoint Method you will start by writing the first chapter, then you will jump to the last chapter and, after that, you will turn your attention to the waypoint chapters. This way you will have a clear sense of where you are going. You will not get lost when you start writing the in-between chapters.

Writing Chapter 1

Let's assume you've settled down at your computer, have made yourself a cup of coffee and you have your character descriptions and your novel's route map alongside you.

You're ready to start writing Chapter 1.

The first page will be your cover page. Although it's not absolutely necessary at this stage of the game, I would suggest you start with it anyway. It will become essential later when you submit the completed novel to an agent or publisher. The page will show your personal details, the title, the word count and the genre. You won't know your exact word count at this stage, but you can add that later. Alternatively, you could write down the figure that you're aiming at until you get the final count.

The cover page should be set out like this:

Darley Chickens
Bleak House
Barchester
Midlandshire
Tel: 01234 56789
Email: darley.c@darleyc.com
Website: www.darleychickensbooks.com

A Tale of Two Places
by
Darley Chickens
83,500 words
Genre: Romance

Next, you should add the page numbers. Although MS Word (in tune with other software) has some fancy pagination options, a simple page number at the bottom of the page is all you need.

Now you're ready to write the words 'Chapter 1' at or near the top of page 2 and get started. Well, you're almost ready. There is one important thing you must now get firmly set in your mind. You will probably have decided on it much earlier but, if not, you must think about it now.

Point of view (POV)

Before you begin writing your opening sentence, take a moment to be absolutely clear about the viewpoint you are going to use. If your story switches between various characters, you will probably need to use a third person viewpoint. That's the one where the story is told by an outside narrator who is never identified, and doesn't need to be. The outside narrator will try to get inside the head of each of the story's characters, but will always tell the tale from a physically detached position.

> *Joe walked down the street. He was about to go into the supermarket when he saw Julie coming towards him. He gasped. What was she doing here? She should be at home.*

The important point here is that the narrator is not a part of that story. He's telling it from a detached viewpoint, and yet... and yet he's seeing things as Joe sees them. He's also telling us what Joe is wondering. That's what we mean by 'getting inside the head' of the character. It's something I'll explain in more detail later.

If one main character is present in every scene, you have the option to use the first person viewpoint. That's where the whole novel is told by an 'I' character, someone who is a part of the story. Using the brief clip above, it would read as:

I walked down the street. I was about to go into the supermarket when I saw Julie coming towards me. I gasped. What was she doing here? She should be at home.

There are several advantages to using this viewpoint:

1. It's much easier get into the 'I' character's thoughts and ideas. The reader is getting the narrative straight from the horse's mouth, so to speak. It's like listening to a friend telling you all about what happened to her. For example:

A jolt of fear ran through me when he came into the room. He leered at me and I struggled to my feet, intent on walking out before he got any closer.

2. It brings events into much sharper focus because we feel we are there with the storyteller. For example:

Shivers ran up my spine when he headed straight towards me. I told him after the divorce never to come near me again and yet there he was, rapidly eating up my personal space! I swept my gaze around the room, desperately searching for an easy way out.

Creating that same sense of tension when you write in third person can be done, but it is far from easy.

3. It's easier to hide things from the reader, saving revelations until they have a major impact. Nothing is

lost if the 'I' character doesn't tell all at the beginning, but much can be gained later.

4. It's easier to maintain a continuity of style. Once you get going with the 'I' character's way of relating the story, it's relatively straightforward to continue with that style right to the end.

Be careful with whatever POV you choose. When a story is written in third person, author intrusion can sometimes spoil it. Author intrusion is when the author's opinions and ideas come through too loudly in the way the story is narrated. One way of avoiding this when describing the nature of a particular character is the careful use of dialogue. The character's personality should show through in the way he/she speaks. It becomes a part of the 'show not tell' technique.

A story written in first person also needs very careful thought because the narrator is now one of the characters within the story. We must find additional ways of giving the reader a picture of that character beyond simple description. It is not acceptable in modern literature for the 'I' character to tell us, the readers, that he is kind-hearted and articulate. There must be a way of showing it. Behaviour and dialogue will do much of it, of course, but what about the over-arching way the story is told? It, too, should reflect the nature of the person telling it. Classic examples are *Huckleberry Finn* and *Forrest Gump*. Look at the way those stories are told and *the style of narration* tells you a lot about the 'I' characters.

Where one character does not appear in every scene, it is possible to write the chapters in different first person viewpoints. You could have Chapter 1 with Joe as the 'I' character and Chapter 2 with Julie as the 'I' character. Yes, it can be done, but I don't advise it for a beginner. The personality of each 'I' character must shine through very strongly in order to ensure the reader always knows who is telling that part of the story.

It's also possible to have some chapters written in the third person interspersed with others written in the first person. I used this technique in *The Legacy of Conflict*, using a third person viewpoint for contemporary chapters and a first person viewpoint when telling long-ago history. It worked because the historical elements were based on the discovery of one character's personal history. If you want to try it, be sure that you have a very good reason for it.

Often, when writing in the third person, the writer will want to advance the story through the viewpoints of two characters. That can be done quite easily, but it is important to keep the viewpoints separate. Take this example:

> *Jim was in a quandary as he entered the room. Should he openly admit his indiscretion and come straight out with the truth? Jenny could see that he had something on his mind and she had a good idea what it was. At first Jim tried to hide the truth from her. He was determined he wasn't going to be the first to raise the subject.*

Whose viewpoint are we following in this sequence? The answer is we are seeing things through the viewpoints of both characters. The sequence begins in Jim's viewpoint: *Jim was in a quandary as he entered the room. Should he openly admit his indiscretion and come straight out with the truth?*

It then switches to Jenny's viewpoint: *Jenny could see that he had something on his mind and she had a good idea what it was.*

And then it comes back to Jim's viewpoint again: *At first Jim tried to hide the truth from her. He was determined he wasn't going to be the first to raise the subject.*

Switching between viewpoints like that is not a good idea. It can confuse the reader. You can overcome this problem by first ensuring you tell us all you need to relate in Jim's viewpoint. Stick with Jim and let the reader know what he sees and what he thinks until you have no more to tell us in that viewpoint — for the moment. Then use a section break (i.e. press your 'enter' key twice to introduce a visual break in the text) or introduce a chapter break. Following that, you can switch to Jenny's viewpoint and tell us all that she sees, hears and thinks. It must, however, be apparent from the start of each section — or chapter — whose viewpoint you are following. One way of doing this is to introduce the viewpoint character's name in the opening sentence. For example:

> *Jim stared at his wife and wondered what she was planning next. How was she going to punish him for what he had done? He began to tremble with anticipation.*

Those opening sentences show us that this sequence is in Jim's viewpoint. We are looking inside his head and we see what he is thinking. More will now follow in Jim's viewpoint as we explore his version of events. The confrontation between the characters will be told from Jim's point of view. At the end of the sequence, we can introduce a section break or chapter break and begin the next sequence with:

> *Jenny turned away and gritted her teeth. What on earth made him think he could get away with that? Well, she would soon show him what she thought of him.*

We are now in Jenny's viewpoint, seeing inside her head, and this is obvious from the start of the sequence. The rest of that section of the story must now continue in Jenny's viewpoint. We can now follow her reaction to the confrontation, seeing inside her head.

You should now be clear about the viewpoint(s) you are about to use in Chapter 1. The next point for you to consider is the form of words you will use to open that chapter. This will be very important. Apart from your synopsis, it will probably be the first thing an agent or publisher reads.

The opening sentence

Have you any ideas for an opening sentence that will capture the reader's imagination? Can you think of words that will get your reader hooked right from the start? Give it some thought now, but don't worry if it doesn't come to you straightaway. I rarely have those 'killer' words in my head when I start on Chapter 1. I'll usually come back to it later, when my subconscious mind has had time to dwell on it. I've even woken up in the night with an opening sentence alive inside my head. So, it may take a while before you come up with a good opening.

But it will have to be good, really good.

At a writers' conference I attended, an agent was asked, "When you read a three-chapter submission, how long does it take you to decide whether to ask for the rest of the manuscript?" His reply was, "I've invariably decided by the end of the first page. Sometimes by the end of the first paragraph. Just occasionally, I have been hooked by the opening sentence." My reaction was to wonder why he wanted three chapters, but that's by the by.

It shouldn't surprise you that an agent will look to be hooked by the opening page — even if you, like me, are wondering why they ask for three chapters. Imagine you are that agent sitting at your desk with a dozen or more manuscripts just delivered for you to assess. That's today's mail, and there will be another lot delivered tomorrow. You don't have time to digest every one of those manuscripts in detail, so you're going to read each one up to the point where you lose interest in it. Frequently, that point will be reached by the end of the first page. Often sooner.

The message here is stark and simple: you've got to capture the reader's attention right at the start.

Your opening sentence(s) will have to grab the reader, like shark's teeth, and not let go. It has to be a 'killer' opening. The best writers always knew that. By 'killer' I don't mean that someone has to be stabbed to death in the first line, far from it. I mean the words must make a deep impression and stick in the reader's mind. They can be loud words or soft words, but always memorable. It's the sort of opening that will drag the reader's thoughts back to that book again and again. Here are a few examples:

> "It was a bright cold day in April and the clocks were striking thirteen." (*1984* by George Orwell)
>
> "It is a truth universally acknowledged that a single man in possession of a good fortune must be in need of a wife." (*Pride and Prejudice* by Jane Austen)
>
> "Scarlett O'Hara was not beautiful, but men seldom realised it when caught by her charm." (*Gone With the Wind* by Margaret Mitchell)

> "When I was small I would sometimes dream of a city — which was strange because it began before I even knew what a city was." (*The Chrysalids* by John Wyndham)
>
> "It was the day my grandmother exploded." (*The Crow Road* by Iain Banks)
>
> "They shoot the white girl first." (*Paradise* by Toni Morrison)
>
> "For a man of his age, fifty-two, divorced, he has, to his mind, solved the problem of sex rather well." (*Disgrace* by J.M. Coetzee)
>
> "My mother did not tell me they were coming." (*Girl with a Pearl Earring* by Tracy Chevalier)
>
> "I did almost nothing on my first day as Idi Amin's doctor." (*The Last King of Scotland* by Giles Foden)

You'll surely have your favourites and be able to quote them easily. If you are unable to think of a killer opening at this stage, make a mental note to think about it and go back to the opening later.

Dialogue

Dialogue is also going to be important. A bit of dialogue on page one will visually break up the text and make it look less demanding for the reader. That's a very subtle psychological point, but one for you to consider now. A page of dense description at the start of a novel can work if it is brilliant writing, but you will help things along if you try to avoid it.

If you think you're weak in constructing dialogue, work at

it. The dialogue you put in the mouths of your characters must be there for a reason. It should either advance the plot, or tell us something important about the characters. Sometimes dialogue can tell us more than the narrative.

Imagine that you glance at a novel in a bookshop and the opening page contains this short conversation.

"That's not right."
"Oh dear. I shall have to do it again."

What does this tell you about the characters? Are they men or women? What nationality are they? What do you know about their temperament? Well, actually, you know little if anything about them. Quite frankly, you probably don't even care about them. Now compare that dialogue with this:

"Jeez! Can't you goddamn Limeys do anything right?"
"I say, old chap. No need to get shirty, you know. I'll jolly well have another go at it."

Now you know a lot more because of what they said and how they said it. You know that one character is an American man and he's distinctly unhappy. The other character is probably an upper-crust Englishman who doesn't like the way he's been addressed. Just a few lines of dialogue tell us so much. We also know that there is going to be conflict between them from the outset. These people come to life as a direct result of their dialogue.

Let's take another example. Suppose this dialogue exchange appears somewhere in the opening page of a romantic novel:

"Would you like to go to the cinema with me?"
"That would be very nice."

"We could go out for a meal if you prefer."
"I'd rather we saw a film."

What do you know about these two? Once again, the answer is: almost nothing. It's all very bland and inconsequential. Does it advance the plot? Not a lot, apart from telling us that the girl doesn't want to dine out with the guy. Not yet, anyway. Do you care about the people? Probably not. So let's look at a different dialogue exchange:

"Hey, Gorgeous! Fancy meetin' me later, do yer?"
"You again? Oh, all right. Meet me outside the 'Ammersmiff Odeon at seven."
"Nah! Seen that film. 'Ow about a Big Mac instead?"
"On yer bike!"

That's a bit more lively. You now know the setting is London and the characters are probably working class or lower middle class. The girl sounds intriguing. She certainly won't be a pushover. It would be interesting to find out more about her motivations. So here we get a better mental image of the two people and their backgrounds. We also get the first stirrings of the girl's attitude towards the boy. And, more than that, the whole scene comes to life.

Character behaviour

Along with the dialogue, you should now be giving a lot of thought towards the way in which your characters behave. This is going to strongly tax your imagination. Your characters' behaviour should be based upon their motivations. It's up to you to decide what will motivate them, based upon your preparation work. *How* you reveal that motivation may not be so easily determined. It may come to light as part of a backstory to which you will have to refer in the narrative. If more detail is needed, you may have to relate it in flashback. Or it may be something that happens within your opening chapter(s).

In his book *The Kite Runner*, Khaled Hosseini describes how his key character goes on a dangerous mission into Afghanistan to rescue a child. What motivates that character? Hosseini uses *half of the book* to detail that motivation which stems from the character's own childhood in Kabul. It's a fascinating story because we understand what the key character feels and experiences throughout the book. When it comes to the later crunch chapters, we understand his motivation.

The main risk you run when you write your book is that you gloss over the things that motivate your main character's behaviour. By all means keep your outline notes basic and unemotional but, when you get to this stage of writing the story, you should make sure your reader fully understands *why* that character behaves as he or she does. It will help you bring things to life.

'Showing' versus 'telling'

This is a suitable moment to look at the techniques of 'showing' and 'telling'. A lot of people have problems understanding the distinction between these two techniques, but it's actually quite straightforward. 'Showing', rather than 'telling', is another way of getting under a character's skin.

You can *tell* us that a character was angry:
She was angry.

Or you can *show* us:
She raised her fists and screamed an obscenity.

You can *tell* us a character is afraid of her ex-husband:
She was afraid of her ex-husband.

Or you can *show* us:
She stiffened as soon as he entered the room, tightening her grasp on her glass. Memories of all he had done to her flooded back into her mind. The pain, the torment! She flinched when the glass cracked in her hand. Blood trickled across her palm and onto the floor.

You can *tell* us a character didn't like his boss:
He didn't like his boss.

Or you can *show* us:
Tension rippled through him whenever his boss confronted the office clerks. He kept his gaze lowered to his desk, hoping he would not be singled out for criticism. But he knew it was a forlorn hope. If only he was strong enough to say what he thought, strong enough to shout back.

Look at those examples again and make sure you can see the fundamental difference between 'showing' and 'telling'. One is a basic statement of what is happening. The other is an insight into the character's behaviour that gives us a vivid picture of what's going on. Once you've grasped the knack of it, you'll find it easy to use the 'showing' technique whenever appropriate.

There will be occasions when 'telling' is useful, though. For example, it's a helpful way to condense events which are not important to your story as such, but which the reader nonetheless needs to know. Having said this, the 'showing' technique is very powerful and you should aim to use it whenever you can. It will bring a scene to life and make the readers feel they're right there with your characters.

Let's take a moment to explore the subject of 'showing' and 'telling' in more depth. So far, I have described these techniques in terms of one or the other. That's a good way to start looking at the techniques. But, in fact, there is a gradation between the two absolutes of totally showing and totally telling. In his book, *The Art of Fiction*, John Gardner describes the differences as 'psychic distance'. I prefer to think of it as a sliding scale that stretches between totally telling and totally showing.

Here are some examples:

Totally telling

On the first day of the Second World War, a trainee pilot panicked when he got lost over the south coast of England.

That's a clear and absolute statement. The reader is being told something in a factual way. It could almost be non-fiction in the way it is related.

Mostly telling

Pilot Officer Peter Norland gripped the Spitfire's stick tightly and wondered where he was.

That's a step forward from the purely factual statement. The reader is still being told what is happening, but that tight grip on the stick gives us a hint of 'showing' in terms of his rising panic.

Telling and showing

Norland felt the bile rise in his mouth as he gripped the stick tighter still. Where was he? He hadn't a clue.

In this example, we're still being *told* what is happening, but the taste of bile and the tighter grip *shows* us that the pilot is beginning to panic. The question at the end takes us further into his thoughts.

Mostly showing

Sweat dribbled down beneath his collar as Pilot Officer Norland frantically searched for a recognisable part of the coastline. A stabbing pain ran across his forehead. If only he knew where he was.

That's better. Now we're really getting deeper into the pilot's thoughts.

Totally showing

His heart pounded. He didn't want to die down there in the emptiness of that grey-green landscape. But where the hell was he? Pain stabbed through his hands as they grasped the stick even tighter. If only he could find just one recognisable landmark. If only! The pounding sensation reached up into his head. God, get me out of this!

Now we're really inside the pilot's thoughts, seeing the situation as he experienced it. We're being shown his panic in graphic detail.

It will be up to you to decide how you describe each scene in your novel. My advice is to use the full-blown showing technique primarily for your main characters. The actions of minor characters — those who belong firmly in the background — would probably be better served by shifting the balance closer to the telling side. You don't want your minor characters to overshadow the main characters.

Here's a little exercise to check your understanding of telling and showing. Which of these examples is totally showing and which is totally telling?

1. Mike caught the last bus home. His wife gave him hell.

2. Sally clenched her fists and drew a deep breath. "How dare you, Mike!" she hissed through clenched teeth. "I told you not to come back here! I don't want to see you in this house ever again!"

3. Jim swung his car into the fast lane and rammed his foot to the floor. He had less than ten minutes to get to the church.

4. Tina held her arms wide, an unmistakable tingle rippling through her. "Oh, Jim, I thought you'd never get here," she whispered. She flung herself into his arms with a sudden burst of tears filling her eyes. "Oh God, I'm so glad. So very glad. I thought you'd never make it in time!"

In examples 1 and 3, the writer is telling us, in simple language, what is happening. The scene is not entirely clear because we're not getting under the characters' skin, not experiencing their emotions.

In examples 2 and 4, however, we're right there with the characters, being shown how Sally and Tina feel. Nowhere in example 2 can we see the word 'angry' and yet we know full well that Sally is angry because we're being *shown* it. Nowhere in example 4 can we see the words 'happy' or 'joyful', but we know that's exactly how Tina feels because we're being *shown* it.

Get in late — get out early

In the 19th and early 20th centuries, novelists had no competition from radio or television and little competition from cinemas. Novels written in that era usually began at a slow pace. They could afford to because the reader was not going to put the book away in order to watch *Eastenders* or *The Simpsons.* The Victorian or Edwardian reader accepted the slow start as a norm and was willing to work through an opening chapter which was little more than scene-setting.

This will not work today.

If you do not capture your readers' attention early, you will lose them. They will put the book aside and switch on the television. That is why you need a killer opening. I've mentioned that earlier. You also need to heed the maxim of 'get in late — get out early'. It's something that should encapsulate every scene in your book, and especially the opening one. Let's see what it means.

You should already have your outline plan, so let's imagine you are about to write an opening chapter based upon this:

Jenny walked down a narrow country road.

She felt happy because she had a new dress.

She admired the country scenery.

She greeted various people with a friendly smile.

She popped into the dress shop again.

She came out and saw smoke and flames coming from the vicarage.

Where will you begin that scene? Will you describe the countryside Jenny walks through? Will you tell us all about Jenny's happy frame of mind? Will you describe her dress? Will you bring in the various people Jenny meets as she strolls along? Will you lead us through the dialogue between Jenny and those people?

No.

It may have worked one hundred years ago, but it will not work today. You will almost certainly lose your reader straightaway. Think about that busy literary agent with a dozen or more submissions in front of him. He wants to cut straight to the opening hook. If you drift along with inconsequential matters, he will quickly toss aside your masterpiece. Which is a pity because it could be a brilliant story once it gets going.

Begin with the action: the smoke and flames coming from the vicarage.

It was a good job the vicar was married to a decent woman, Jenny thought. It was the only thing that kept her lust in check. She smiled to herself as she strode out of Mrs Higgins' dress shop into the quiet village street. The afternoon sunshine suddenly dazzled her, making her blink. As her eyes began to refocus, she stopped abruptly.

"Oh, my God!" She threw a hand to her mouth and stared at the vicarage, directly across the road. Smoke and flames were pouring from the library window. Was the vicar in there? Would he be hurt?

That's what we mean by 'get in late'. The opening takes the reader straight into the action... along with an insight into Jenny's thoughts. I have abbreviated the scene because this is only an illustration. You could embroider it more than I have, but the principle remains. Start with something that is going to grab your readers' attention. Make them want to read on to find out what happens next.

Now let's look at the ending to that scene. Here's your outline plan:

Jenny ran back into the shop.

She asked Mrs Higgins to call the fire brigade.

She ran across the road to the vicarage, hoping everyone would get out.

The vicar came hurrying out.

"Thank God, you're safe," said Jenny. "But where's your wife?"

The vicar didn't know.

The house was now ablaze.

They waited for the fire brigade to come.

They discussed where the vicar's wife might be.

They watched the vicarage burning.

Mrs Higgins came out to join them.

At what point will you end that scene? By getting in late, you have captured your readers' attention, but you now need to hold onto it. You want your readers to keep reading, so don't allow the tension to flag. Look for the cliff-hanger point and end the scene there.

The house was now ablaze.

That's the point where you end the scene. A point of high drama. And you now have a couple of good options. You could cut straight to Chapter 2, knowing your readers will want to turn the page in order to find out what happens next. Maybe Chapter 2 will begin with a fireman discovering a body. Or you could introduce a section break and take us to a different scene with different characters, leaving the readers wondering about the vicar's wife. It's a literary tease. The readers have to read on until they rejoin the drama scene in the village. It's the only way they will find out if the vicar's wife survives.

Writing the ending

You have the prospect of an unwritten novel stretching out in front of you. Even for experienced writers, writing that novel can be a daunting undertaking. That's where the Waypoint Method can lighten the psychological load. You'll still have to write the book, but the task will seem much less formidable if you do it this way.

Many years ago, when I was learning to fly, I was taught the saying: "If you know where you've come from and you know where you're going to, you will never be lost. At worst, you may be temporarily unsure of your position, but you will never be completely lost."

Think about that in terms of the novel you are writing. *Where you've come from* is the opening chapter. *Where you're going to* is the closing chapter. If you can get those two points set in concrete (or at least reasonably secured into the format you are aiming for), you need never be lost. Isn't that a comforting thought?

I have already shown you how to prepare a route map of the entire novel and you should have it in front of you now. You should also know your characters because you designed them and guided them through Chapter 1. So, what's to stop you from writing the ending of the book? Later, in the editing stage, you may choose to make some small adjustments to the final chapter — let's call it tweaking — but you will not need to scrap the work you do now.

There are various sorts of novel endings. Let's look at a few of them:

1. The *'I didn't see that coming'* ending

This is the ending that catches you unawares and, yet, when you think back over the story, it was inevitable all along. The clues were hidden, but they existed. It is the sort of ending you cannot make up off the cuff when you get to the last page. Try making it up at the last minute and it may well look contrived and out of place. The clues have to be carefully planted in the manuscript at salient points so that the end doesn't look false. This is where the Waypoint Method works in your favour. If you choose to write an unexpected ending now, you will be able to paint in the small clues when you come to write the intermediate chapters. It should all fit together smoothly. I used this kind of ending in my novel, *The Legacy of Conflict*, and only revealed the identity of who had been hanged on Warlock Hill at the end of the novel. I was able to fit in the salient clues at strategic points because I knew exactly how the plot was going to pan out.

2. The *poignant* ending

This is the sort of ending that leaves the emotional reader

close to tears. It's a sad ending but a satisfying one if it is the only conclusion that fits neatly into the plot. Maybe the key character dies and the remaining characters are left bereaved. They gather at the grave and mourn their loss. Maybe the girl doesn't get the man she loves because she realises he loves someone else more than he loves her. She walks away with a trembling chin, knowing she is doing the right thing. It is an ending that has to be handled carefully to ensure that the emotions come across in a believable manner. You want a classic example? How about *A Tale of Two Cities*? A man gives up his life for the sake of the woman he loves and the man she loves. How else could Dickens have satisfyingly ended the story?

3. The *'all-wrapped up'* ending

This is where you have no twist in the tale, no cause for tears, just a straight winding-up of the story that sees all the threads neatly explained. It doesn't mean the ending lacks emotion. On the contrary, it can be quite dramatic, but most of all it should be conclusive. Many writers find this a difficult ending to write because they don't know when to stop. Should they go on a few more pages? Should they explain everything in absolutely precise detail, like Hercule Poirot gathering together all the suspects and revealing who did it and how he teased out all the clues? The most common error is to drag out the ending too long. Earlier, I mentioned a technique known as 'Get in late — get out early'. I said that 'getting in late' meant starting with the first action scene. 'Getting out early' means ending the story before you start boring your readers with unnecessary waffle. The two main characters have finally got it together. Stop there. Don't tell us about their new life in a quaint little cottage in the woods with roses around the door. That's waffle and it spoils the ending.

4. The *'something still to tell'* ending

Sometimes called the 'open-ended' conclusion, this is often a difficult one to write. Just because everything is not fully explained there is no reason why it cannot be a satisfying ending. There are two basic types of 'open-ended' novels. There is the one-off book with a major aspect of the plot left to the reader's imagination. The device should not be frustrating for the reader: it should leave him thinking, pondering over the underlying message. The satisfaction will lie in the reader's ability to come to his or her own conclusions. Then there is the novel series where it is important for the author to leave certain plot elements incomplete so that the readers will come back and read the rest of the books in the series. Did Richard Sharpe survive the Peninsular War? We don't know until we get to the end of the series. Did Sophie Kinsella's shopaholic eventually overcome her addiction? You have to read the series to find out.

5. The *epilogue* ending

This can be a useful device, but only if it is handled with care. It comes into its own when the story conclusion must be told in a time frame that comes after the final chapter has ended. I used it to effect in *The Legacy of Conflict*. The final chapter sees all the loose ends neatly up, or so the reader is left to think. I could have ended the book at that point, but I didn't. I added an epilogue which, at a stroke, changed the whole dénouement. This was the ending I planned all along, but I led the reader along a false path before getting to it. I like to think it works as an epilogue and as a plot line.

Whichever sort of ending you use, it must be satisfying to the readers. By 'satisfying', I mean that the readers should have enjoyed the book and may even be disappointed at coming to the end of it. In other words, the ending has appealed to their emotions in a way that leaves them wanting more. That doesn't mean there should be more pages to overcome the disappointment of reaching the last page. It means there should be more of your novels on the bookshop shelves for them to buy.

The reader's satisfaction could come from seeing the main character overcome the problems you put in the way at the start of the novel. It could come from a feeling of relief that the good guys won over the bad guys. It could come from the feeling of pleasure that the girl won her boy. It must always come about as a result of the way in which you describe the final events.

Writing the middle part of the novel

You now have your opening chapter and your final chapter. These two chapters are not perfect — not yet — but the whole story is well structured. You know where you started and you know where you are heading. You are now about to venture into the middle section of your story, the bridge over which your characters must cross: the bridge between the opening chapter that sets up the whole story, and the closing chapter that ties things up. This is the part of the book — the lengthy part of the book — where your main characters must go through a process of change. Shortly, I will introduce the matter of waypoint chapters which you will write next, but first you need to understand more about *how* your characters will change in the course of the plot.

Your main character should change

Go back to that girl I told you about in *The Legacy of Conflict*, the one who went from supremely nasty to admirable heroine in the space of 29 chapters. I had to engineer the change so that it looked real to the reader. A sudden unexpected change was never going to work, so I had to pay attention to three aspects of what I wrote about that girl in the middle part of the book.

1. The reader had to understand *why* she was the way she was at the start of the story. What were her motivations? What was her background? I had to bring in a back-story to explain her actions, even bring a sense of logic to those actions. Those scenes had to be written very carefully. It wasn't enough just to say, "She did this because of that." I had to make the reader see things from her point of view so that doing 'this' because of 'that' had a sense of inevitability about it.

2. The reader had to see that she was capable of change *in the right circumstances*. I had to create those circumstances by taking her away from her abusive environment and by giving her a role model she could copy. Those two devices put in place the opportunity for change, but I had to show the reader that the girl was actually capable of taking the chances as they opened up to her. Change didn't come to her easily and it didn't come to her quickly. In real life it rarely does. She needed some prodding along the way. The plot devices were written into the route map early on, but the way I explained them came as a result of much deliberation. I

had to see inside the girl's head, to show her initial reluctance to make such a leap of faith, to show her gradual realisation that she had an opportunity that might never come again, to show her slowly accepting a new way... and then to show her final understanding that this was what she actually wanted. This was her new life and she would never turn back.

3. I had to show the reader that the girl's new life was plausible. It would never have worked had I put the girl into a new situation she was quite incapable of handling. With that in mind, I made her strong right from the start, and I made her a fighter. She had her moments of doubt and depression because of what happened in the backstory, but she was, at heart, the sort of person who was able to move on. All she needed was that chance and the role model to show her the way.

There must be logic in the way your characters behave. There must be a reason behind their behaviour. I mentioned Elizabeth Bennet earlier. She changes her attitude towards Mr Darcy as the story of *Pride and Prejudice* develops, and her change is a logical extension of her character and behaviour. Firstly, she is the sort of intelligent, thinking woman who would be prepared to see a different side of Mr Darcy, and capable of accepting that new impression of him in good faith. Had she been dogmatic or heavily biased, it wouldn't have worked. Secondly, she has a sense of moral goodness that allows her to empathise with Mr Darcy's ethical and generous behaviour when her sister runs away with Wickham. It was all a logical extension of the way Elizabeth's character was designed by Jane Austen. Make no mistake about it, Jane was a writer who knew exactly what she was doing.

In order to make the key character's change seem real, you will need to think carefully about the clues you dish out along the way. Think carefully, also, about the clues to the final dénouement. The rule is: not too many, not too few. And we're not necessarily talking about crime stories here.

In my novel *The Legacy of Secrets*, a man is beset with nightmare visions of things that happened in World War II, a conflict that ended well before he was born. What do those nightmares mean? Why does he see them? All is revealed in the final chapters and the solution has a logical inevitability about it. Everything leads up to that single possible answer. But I had to plant some subtle clues along the way.

Suppose I had dropped just one clue somewhere in the middle. The reader would likely have felt cheated and asked, "Just that one tiny clue? How on earth was I supposed to pick up on that?" Alternatively, suppose I had set down blatant markers in every chapter. Again, the reader would have felt cheated because the answer would be too obvious, too soon. "The book was spoiled because I saw the end coming long before I reached it."

It was a very fine balance of throwing in clues at strategic points without making the point of the story too clear too soon. One single clue was not enough. I had to introduce several, and they had to fit together like a jigsaw with the final piece falling into place near the end of the book.

Think carefully, also, about the nature of your antagonists, who may well be villains. They will not change as the story progresses, but the way you describe them and their character flaws will be important. Just as your key character will have a reason for his or her flaws, so will your villains.

It's best if you don't turn your villain(s) into a comic book caricature like Captain Hook or the Joker. More importantly, a villain should be villainous *for a reason*. In other words, he should have his motivations just as your hero and heroine have their motivations. His motives may be questionable to you, but they should be real to him.

In *The Legacy of Conflict* I introduce two villains, one in the current time and one in the 17th century. The present-day villain is an IRA bomber. His motivations are centred upon his hatred of anything British, something he learned through growing up in a staunchly republican environment. The historical villain is an English Protestant soldier, one of Cromwell's generals. His motivations are centred upon his hatred of Catholic Royalists, something that sprang from the murder of his wife in the Irish Rising of 1641. My readers are not expected to like either of them, but they should understand what made the villains the way they are. Neither of them acts out of pure, unadulterated evil intent. They do their bad deeds because of internal motivations that are meaningful to them.

The waypoint chapters

Now you are in a position to write the intermediate waypoint chapters which will encompass those character changes.

Your novel will have a beginning, a middle and an end. You've written the beginning of the beginning — Chapter 1 — and you've written the end — the final chapter. You know that the story starts at the right place and it finishes at the right place and in the right manner. Think sandwich: the very beginning and very end are the slices of bread and you're now ready to put the filling between those slices.

Well, actually, it isn't quite like that because your sandwich is going to have two more slices of bread within the outer ones. Call it a club sandwich. We're going to call the extra slices of bread the waypoint chapters.

Even though you know your starting point and your end point, it is possible to become temporarily unsure of your position along the way. You are now about to minimise that risk. Look at your chapter-by-chapter route map and identify two suitable chapters, one about a third of the way into the story and the other about two thirds of the way. It's shouldn't be difficult to pick out these chapters, but you should be swayed towards writing scenes that are crucial turning points in the plot. Can you identify points where the action absolutely must run rigidly along certain lines? If you can write those chapters now, you are further casting the plot in stone. Everything else must now fit in between the four chapters you will have on your computer: the start and end chapters, and the two waypoint chapters.

Let's take an example you should be able to relate to. You are Jane Austen and you are writing *Pride and Prejudice*. You have completed the first chapter and the last chapter. You know what you have to do next and you're nicely seated at your 18th century steam-driven computer. The CPU boiler is fully stoked and the screen is flickering with its candle illumination.

Your fingers hover over the cast iron keyboard. Which chapters are you going to write? Volume 1, Chapter 16 sees Wickham, the rogue, denounce Mr Darcy in front of Elizabeth. This is an important part of the plot. It details Wickham's supposed loss of inheritance and sets bare his dislike of Darcy. So this would be a suitable chapter to use as the first waypoint.

Volume 3, Chapter 1, sees Elizabeth at Pemberley along

with her aunt and uncle. This is the chapter in which Elizabeth sees Mr Darcy in his own grand house for the first time. She learns from the housekeeper a deeper insight into the man, and then she meets him in the garden. Slowly, her feelings for him begin to change. It's a turning point suitable to be the second waypoint.

So, you write these two chapters.

Think of these as mini-stories in their own right. They won't be complete in themselves, but they will carry forward your plot. Aim to encompass all the emotion and action you've planned in your route map, but don't worry that there will be no conclusive end to them. In fact, you may well want to finish each of them on a cliff-hanger.

After that, all that's left is the task of filling in the bits in between. In that task, you will find yourself using all the techniques I have so far described.

The hard slog and the motivation to keep on writing

If you have a first chapter, a last chapter and two waypoint chapters, you will probably have written somewhere between eight and twelve thousand words. Let's compromise on, say, ten thousand. There is a likelihood that you will eventually end up with around one hundred thousand words. Maybe more, maybe less. One hundred thousand seems to be the average for my novels, in which case those ten thousand words represent just one tenth of the novel. A small fraction, but a very important fraction.

So, now we come to the 'perspiration' part of the writing, the bit that's going to take up most of your time. The story is going to work, you know that because you've got everything planned, but it's going to take some effort to complete it. Not as much as if you were writing off the cuff, but serious effort all the same.

With the best will in the world, you are going to meet spells when you will experience some lack of motivation. It happens to all of us, so don't look upon the experience as abnormal. It isn't. There are times when I stagger into my study in the morning, switch on my computer with good intentions and then glance out the window to see the sun shining brightly. That's when my motivation can begin to flag. It's a beautiful warm day and I just want to be out there lazing on the garden seat with a cup of tea in one hand and the daily paper in the other. Ah, bliss. But that isn't going to get my latest novel finished. I know what I ought to be writing — the novel that's firmly set out in my plan — but then a dose of lethargy sets in.

It's probably going to happen to you, and these are the moments when you can go in one of two ways. You can give up, succumb to your leisurely instincts and turn off your computer... or you can motivate yourself to continue writing.

Now heed this: giving up is the worst option. It might not seem like that at the time, but you will regret it later.

There are four prime reasons why you might lose motivation.

1. You lose confidence. You don't think the story is going to work so you might as well give up now.

2. You lose focus. You've lost the picture of what you wanted out of this story. It all seems to have gone fuzzy. Why are you writing this thing anyway?

3. You lose direction. You don't know what should happen next in your story. You meet the brick wall.

4. You become mentally lethargic. Something else seems more attractive.

Look carefully at the first three of those four reasons and you should be able to spot a bright light shining through. By the very fact of your planning process, you have already mitigated against them, all three of them. You cannot totally eliminate the chance of losing your motivation through any one of those three reasons, but you can reduce the chances to manageable levels. *And you have already done that.* You have reduced the chance of losing confidence, focus or direction because your story plan will carry you through. You know already that your story will work.

The only thing that may now get in your way is that age old enemy... lethargy. It's that state of tiredness or mental fatigue that makes you want to go back to bed and forget all about writing.

Let's suppose that, like me, you occasionally meet that lethargic moment when you just want to switch off your computer and forget all about writing. What can you do to reinvigorate and motivate yourself back into action?

One technique that works is to put up a Motivational Highlighter on the wall beside your computer. It can take the form of a whiteboard, a pinboard or just a big sheet of paper. Something you can use to highlight the value of keeping going. Maybe it's just a sheet of paper with a few motivational quotes. There are many of them out there waiting for you to pick up. Here are a few:

"The way to get started is to quit talking and begin doing."
Walt Disney

"In order to succeed, we must first believe that we can." Nikos Kazantzakis

"Fake it until you make it! Act as if you had all the confidence you require until it becomes your reality." Brian Tracy

When your motivation begins to flag through lethargy, stop and think about those quotes. This is a very simple technique, but some people swear by it. It will do you no harm to try it.

Other people work with punishment and reward notes. They take a blank sheet of paper and jot down a punishment list they will inflict upon themselves if they don't get the job done: no chocolate bars with their tea, no special dinner treat, no day off on Sunday. Or they jot down the rewards they will give themselves if the job is done: a night at the cinema, an expensive dinner, a new coat. It's another technique some people swear by.

The technique I use is much more specific to me and it's not one I ever recommend to others. I'll tell you how it works for me, but it comes with a health warning: if it doesn't work for you, it could leave you depressed.

My novels sell, and that's very nice, but my overriding aim these days is to leave behind something for generations to come, especially for my children and my grandchildren. They are important to me, and my books are a legacy that will be with them when I am long gone from this world. I can picture my two grandsons, fifty years from now, picking up my books and reading them in the knowledge that their grandfather wanted to leave behind something of himself. Something that would last. So, how does that affect my behaviour now? Well, some years ago, I had a major heart attack. I survived it — obviously! — but it was a big wake-up call. It made me realise I am not immortal and, if I want to achieve anything worthwhile in this life, I have to get on and do it. No procrastination, no dithering, just get on and do it. Now. Because one day I won't be there to do it.

When I get those lethargic moments, I ask myself what will be the outcome if I walk away from my latest writing task right now and my life ends tonight. A bit of a gruesome thought, I know, and that's why I don't recommend this idea to others. In that event, I tell myself, I will not be able to complete something I want my descendants to inherit. I will leave this life with a sense of not having achieved something I wanted to do for my family.

That's my motivator. No notices beside my computer, no written notes about punishment or reward, just a simple thought. You might be better advised to try the Motivational Highlighter. It's far less gruesome.

Eventually, after much time and effort, you will complete the novel. We know you will, because you have designed it to work as a well-structured story. What then? What do you do after you've typed the words "THE END"? The answer is easy.

Stop.

Put the whole thing aside and forget about it for a couple of weeks. Yes, a couple of weeks... at least. Leave it for a full month if you can bring yourself to do so. Allow your thoughts to drift away from the manuscript so that you can come back to it later with an open mind. You deserve a pat on the back for getting this far and it's been a long, hard slog. You probably need to relax before you tackle the next stage of the novel's development, the editing process.

STAGE 3
EDITING

STAGE 3
EDITING

First, a quick explanation of what we mean by editing, and how it differs from proofreading.

Editing is all about improving the overall quality of writing so that the end result is fit for purpose and free from any grammatical or typing errors. It means enhancing language use and making sure the content is logical, accurate and without any ambiguities, inconsistencies, repetitions or omissions.

Proofreading comes later. It is what a publisher does before sending the manuscript to a printer. Sometimes the term proofreading is also used to mean checking grammar and spelling, but it is actually the copy editor's job to make sure that the nitty-gritty details are correct. I prefer to understand the term proofreading in its stricter sense: as the process of checking the proofs before books are printed. In this section I will talk primarily about editing.

Many writers — especially hobbyists — will edit their own manuscripts. (I will give you some advice on how to tackle that task shortly.) Some will get family and friends to help with the editing process. Others will get specialist editors to do the work for them.

If you call upon non-professionals — friends or family — to help you get your novel into a publishable format, you may well find that their responses will be based primarily upon personal opinions. They may tell you they like or dislike what you have written, but will not be able to tell you why. "It's just not the sort of story I enjoy," doesn't really help you. A professional editor will be more likely to give you an unbiased response, one that concentrates upon the technical faults which need to be addressed.

In various books and magazines, you will come across the terms 'alpha reader', 'beta reader', 'copy editor' and 'proofreader'. These four titles need some explanation.

The alpha reader

You've completed the first draft and you want an early appraisal of the work. This is where you will offer the manuscript to an alpha reader. He or she may be a professional reader or just a friend. Either way, that person will take a broad overview of the whole novel and will give a general determination of:

Does it hang together as a cohesive story?

Are the characters believable?

Is the setting well drawn?

Is the plot believable?

Does the plot have any major inconsistencies?

The beta reader

You have now taken to heart the comments by the alpha reader and you have made extensive revisions to the manuscript. At this stage, you may be on the third or fourth draft. Now you will hand the manuscript to a beta reader. To begin with, this reader will comment on the exactly same points as the alpha reader but in much more depth. The beta reader's appraisal will assess the story chapter by chapter, page by page, and will determine whether you have cleared up all the inconsistencies discovered by the alpha reader. It is possible, of course, that the beta reader may be the alpha reader wearing a different hat. In that case he/she will know exactly what to look for this time around.

The copy editor

You should now have addressed the beta reader's assessment and corrected all the errors thrown up. The manuscript will be getting close to its final form but there are still two more stages to go through. This is where the copy editor will take over and look at:

Grammar

Spelling

Typing errors

Word usage

Factual errors

Contradictory and/or illogical content

Stylistic inconsistencies

By the time a copy editor has finished his/her work, the manuscript should be clear, correct, coherent, complete, concise, consistent and credible (these are the seven Cs of editing). A good copy editor is worth his/her weight in gold because poor grammar or spelling will immediately mark out your novel as incomplete in the eyes of an agent or publisher. A good copy editor could easily make the difference between success and failure.

The proofreader

As I said earlier, proofreading is what a publisher will do in order to ensure that the proofs that come back from the designer or typesetter are ready for publication. Larger publishing houses will also carry out yet another copy edit at this stage. Smaller presses are more likely to rely upon the commissioning editor's appraisal. In both cases the publisher will always submit the manuscript to a proofreader before it is sent to the printer. This is the person who will carry out the final quality check and tidy-up, including checking the consistency, presentation and accuracy of the text, images and layout. The aim is to make sure that the book is as perfect as it can possibly be. After all, no publisher likes to be accused of publishing a book which is not fully up to marketable standard.

Editing the book yourself

The examples I have shown above work best if those three tasks (alpha, beta and copy editing) are carried out by different people, preferably professional editors. However, employing professional editors can be expensive. Too expensive for some writers. Most new novelists will choose to call upon the services of friends or relatives, or else do the work themselves.

Keep in mind that if you use non-professional alpha readers and beta readers, you must take account of their background. They may well have less understanding of novel-writing techniques than you. Maybe that is why so many writers carry out their own editing, right up to and including the copy-editing stage. Let's assume you are going to do the work yourself. How are you going to tackle those tasks?

My advice is not to begin by following the trail of having three different hats: making yourself an alpha reader, then a beta reader and then a copy editor. For new novelists, that could be confusing. My advice is to give yourself just two different hats. Let's call them the prime-edit hat and the copy-edit hat.

The prime edit

The prime edit is a term I've made up to explain the prime (i.e. first) editing stage. It will involve several read-throughs, so don't assume you'll only need to read the manuscript once at this stage.

The book's finished. It's complete. Or so you think. In fact, you now have an important task in front of you. You must edit it because there is a 99.99% certainty that you will have made some mistakes in the manuscript. We are all human and making mistakes is what we do. They may be simple errors caused by hitting the wrong computer keys, or they may be more significant errors caused by lapses in concentration. But they will exist and you must put them right before an agent or publisher sees the manuscript.

It's a good idea to carry out your prime edit in a different medium to the one you used for writing. In other words, don't do it on your computer. The most common way is to print out the manuscript double-spaced on A4 paper. I've tried that. I've also tried uploading the manuscript onto my Kindle for editing. But my current favourite, and probably most successful way, is to upload it onto an internet book printing site (for example, www.lulu.com) and have a single paperback copy printed. With ink cartridges being so expensive, it can actually work out cheaper than printing the entire novel onto 500 sheets of A4 paper on my home printer. I find, also, that I can pick out mistakes much easier when I'm reading what looks like a finished product. And I can read it in bed or on a bus, which isn't so easy with a desktop computer!

Start the editing process by asking one simple question: does it all make sense? The finished manuscript should be easily understood by you, your characters and your readers. You may understand it, but will your readers? And you must ask yourself if your characters always act in accordance with the viewpoints you present to them.

So, let's look at the manuscript from those three viewpoints. To do this, you will need to think through three different mindsets in order to judge the sense behind the text. That will mean reading the novel at least three times, probably more. I sometimes find I need to go through the entire book half a dozen times before I am happy I have teased out every mistake. Demanding? Yes. Rewarding? Very much so.

1. Your own viewpoint

This is the viewpoint you had when you wrote the manuscript. One important point to consider here is that this is your novel. You planned it, you wrote it, you know what you wanted to achieve. Other people will be able to help you with the editing process, but you are the one best placed to know if the end result measures up to what you wanted to write.

As you read through the text, ask yourself:

> *Do the words say exactly what you meant to say?* Sometimes the words that end up dripping down from your fingertips into the keyboard are not the same as the words you had in our head.
>
> *Do your characters stand out as the sort of people you wanted to create? Is your hero/heroine really the sort of person you wanted him/her to be?*
>
> *Does the action come to life in the way you meant it to come to life?*

Be honest with yourself here. You know what you wanted to write, so is that what you have achieved? If it isn't, this is the time to change it. If something stands out as contrary to what you intended, the changes may need to be significant.

2. Your main character's viewpoint

This is particularly important when you write in a first person singular viewpoint. The words on the page came from you, but they should also reflect what your main character was thinking. Remember what I said earlier about getting under the character's skin. The fact is, you are not your main character, however much you might like to be. Your character will think and act differently to you, and that must be reflected in the manuscript. Try once again to see inside your character's mindset to see if your written words really do reflect his or her thoughts and behaviour. Look out for those glaring continuity errors we are all liable to make, such as the blonde in Chapter 1 who becomes a brunette in Chapter 6. And look out for the man who says, "By gum, lad, that's a right good pint of ale," in Chapter 2, and then says, "What a jolly good idea," in Chapter 10.

3. The reader's viewpoint

This is the really important one. Can your reader enjoy the book? Have you chopped out or corrected anything remotely confusing? You know what you meant when you tapped out those words, but now you must ask yourself if your readers will get the gist of it. We all make mistakes here. We miss out words, or we get them in the wrong order. We think we have written: *he went down the steep stairs.* But the words on the page clearly say: *he down went steep stairs.*

And beware the sin of bad phrasing. We try to write at the speed we think, using the fast-running words in our head. On the page it says: *the school headmaster took a prominent role in the sexual exploitation of the children.* What you meant to write was that the headmaster acted prominently to prevent the exploitation. That's not what was written, and it's probably not what the reader will infer.

Jot down notes on your written copy — as many as you

need in order to indicate what needs to be changed. I like to underline the offending text in red ink and then make explanatory notes in the margin. I don't go back to my computer until I've been right through the manuscript. Then I make the corrections on my Word document.

When you have prime-edited the manuscript, put it aside again for a few days, and then repeat the whole process yet again. I find I need to go through the manuscript at least half a dozen times. In each read-through, I can guarantee you will find a few more errors. More than that, you may discover a few dull patches. Look at the first paragraph again and ask yourself if you can dream up a better killer opening.

If you want to attract an agent or publisher, your first page must sparkle. I don't mean it has to be good because agents get lots of novels sent to them with good opening pages. Yours has to be better than that: it must shine. This is what I call the 'first page test'. If it fails that test, it will not get published. End of story. The rest of the novel may be a winner, but the manuscript can still fail simply because the opening did not shine. So take yourself back to that first page and spend the next few days polishing it until it is brilliant. Not good, but brilliant.

What about the opening sentence. Does it grab the reader? Is it better than anything you've ever read before? Does it outshine *1984* and *Pride and Prejudice*? Be honest with yourself here because an agent is going to give you only one chance at the first page test. Fluff it and you'll end up on the rejection pile.

When you're quite sure you can't do any better, your manuscript should be ready for copy-editing.

The copy edit

The manuscript has now been prime-edited. You've ensured the text makes sense, to you and to your readers. You've ensured the characters act and speak in accordance with their temperament. Surely that's the end of the task, isn't it?

No, prime-editing and copy-editing are not the same thing.

Prime-editing is a way of putting right the author's story-construction errors. It covers the big picture, ensuring the story is easy to follow and the characters are easily understood.

Copy-editing is a way of putting right those awkward nitty-gritty errors that remain, or have crept into, the edited manuscript. They may be spelling errors, grammatical errors or inconsistencies. They have to be put right.

This is not an easy task. The sorts of errors you are now looking for are usually small and easily hidden among the mass of text that surrounds them. You will need to work on the copy-editing in a different way to your method of prime-editing.

Try putting a ruler under each line of text in sequence and read each line in reverse. Sounds daft? Well, actually, it's a method that highlights each word more clearly than simply reading the page in the normal way. You'll find that spelling errors will jump out at you. Surprisingly, other errors will also become easier to spot. But you will need to take your time over this task. If you find your mind drifting away from the text, stop immediately and have a break before you return to it. When you are in doubt about a word or sentence, use a good dictionary or thesaurus. Don't let it pass in the hope that no one will notice if it's wrong.

A word of advice here: never, never, never assume that MS Word will do all your checking for you. Never assume it will pick out every tiny error of grammar or punctuation. It will not. To illustrate the point, I've composed a scene from a story called *A Night with a Knight*. (Don't take the story seriously — it doesn't actually exist, except for this brief extract.)

> *Sir Jasper stared at me with glint's in his eye's.*
> *"Aha! So your awake me dear."*
> *The beds well-worn springs squealed as I sat up. "Your looking sprightly, sir," I said.*
> *"I aint finished with you yet," he replied. "Come 'ere, girl."*
> *He wrapped his arm's around me and...*

Take a moment to count the number of mistakes in that short scene. I put it through MS Word's spelling and grammar checker and this is what came up. It spotted five errors: one spelling mistake and four errors of grammar. I've highlighted them below.

> *Sir Jasper stared at me with glint's in his eye's.*
> *"Aha! So your awake me dear."*
> *The beds well-worn springs squealed as I sat up. "Your looking sprightly, sir," I said.*
> *"I aint finished with you yet," he replied. "Come 'ere, girl."*
> *He wrapped his arm's around me and...*

What are the errors?

First, look at the words with an apostrophe followed by the letter s: *glint's*, *eye's* and *arm's*. An apostrophe like this could mean that the word is a contraction, or it could mean possession. For example, *it's* is a contraction of *it is*, whereas *Jim's book* denotes possession — the book belongs to Jim. *Glint's*, *eye's* and *arm's* are *not* contractions, *nor* do they indicate possession. They are plurals. So there is no need for the apostrophe.

Now take a look at the word *your* in the third line. This is a very common error and one that irritates me. In this context, the word should be *you're*, which is a contraction of *you are.* (*Your* refers to possession.)

Finally, the word *aint* in the fifth line should be *ain't* because it is also derived from a contraction. I say 'derived' because the full version is *am not.* A grammatically accurate sentence would read, *I am not finished with you yet.* It is not grammatically accurate because this is dialogue, using a form of dialect.

So, MS Word spotted those five errors. But here's the important point: there are actually *eight* errors in that short piece. I've underlined the extra three below, the ones the spell-checker didn't spot.

> *Sir Jasper stared at me with glint's in his eye's.*
> *"Aha! So your awake me dear."*
> *The beds well-worn springs squealed as I sat up. "Your looking sprightly, sir," I said.*
> *"I aint finished with you yet," he replied. "Come 'ere, girl."*
> *He wrapped his arm's around me and…*

Why did MS Word pick up only five errors and not eight? I really don't know. It spotted the error with the word *your* in the third line, but the error occurred twice. It occurred in the second line as well as the third. The version of Word that sits on my computer didn't spot that.

Beds, in the third line is also wrong. There should be an apostrophe before the letter s because the word shows possession. The springs belong to the bed.

What is wrong with the word *'ere*? The answer is that the apostrophe at the FRONT of the word — indicating a missing letter — is the wrong way round. It should be *'ere*. That's not an easy mistake for you to pick up, but an experienced editor will spot it straightaway. In order to get the correct direction apostrophe at the FRONT of an abbreviated word, press 'Ctrl' and double-click on the apostrophe key.

If you would like to see what else to look out for when copy-editing, have a look at Appendix C. I've included some more examples there.

The important message is: don't rely upon your computer software to do any editing for you. Do it yourself and do it carefully. If you are struggling with spelling and grammar, use a good dictionary and spend some time studying grammar. It's not that difficult. Your local library is bound to have excellent grammar books you can borrow or you can find grammar websites online. If you have friends who are good at copy-editing, ask if they would be willing to have a look at your manuscript as well.

Copy-editing is not a quick and easy task. It's slow and it demands meticulous attention to the manuscript. But it's worth all the effort it takes.

A further word of advice. A typing error on your first page will tell the agent or publisher that you haven't given enough attention to the editing. When you think you've got the whole thing tied up, go back and tackle the first page again. And again.

STAGE 4
THE FINAL STRETCH

STAGE 4
THE FINAL STRETCH

You've edited your manuscript, so what do you do now? You buy yourself a nice bottle of wine and celebrate. You've earned it. After that, you will probably want to make some firm plans to market your masterpiece. After all, you've put a lot of time and effort into completing the manuscript so it would be foolish to put it in a drawer and forget about it.

What to do with the finished manuscript

Depending on your reason for writing a novel, there are several avenues open to you.

Approaching a literary agent

Most of the major publishing houses will accept novels only through agents, so it's probably not worth approaching the big publishers directly. It's an accepted part of an agent's job to sift out what is obviously not publishable and put forward only those manuscripts that have a chance of success. And they take a chunk of the writer's earning in return for placing it with a publisher. Don't begrudge them that money — they will earn it.

How you approach the agent will vary from person to person. Some like only postal submissions, some like only email submissions and some will accept either. Some will want an introductory letter from you before you submit, and some won't give you a second look unless you are invited to contact them or are recommended to them by a known source. Some are very friendly and helpful while others can be openly abrupt and dismissive. I've chatted to some very courteous agents who have given me valuable advice, and I've been publically humiliated by a rude one. It's just like all human life, really! It's going to be up to you to sort out the good from the bad.

Do your homework by checking each agent's website to find out what they want before you send off your 'begging' letter, with the obligatory three chapters and synopsis. If they say they don't consider multiple submissions (i.e. submissions to several agents at once), ignore it and send off your work to every agent who looks likely to read your particular work. You can't afford to wait around to hear from an agent who may never bother to reply. Believe me, it really does happen: there are agents who don't bother to reply if your work isn't suitable for them.

Approaching a small press

This has been my preferred route to publication. In my experience, most small presses tend not to bother with agents, preferring to work directly with the writers. I have worked with four different companies in the UK and North America and in every case I found them to be helpful and approachable. It's been more like working with friends than dealing with business organisations. The big boys in the publishing industry seem to have less and less time for new and struggling writers and that's where these small presses come into their own. They take on writers who have been otherwise ignored, but are able to deliver good, publishable material.

You'll find lists of small presses online. These companies don't pay out big advances, if any at all, but they will edit, proofread and format your novel, design a front cover and organise its publication. Choose the right small press for your particular novel and you will enjoy the experience. On top of that, you can justly say that you are published by a reputable company. It's a fact that not everyone trusts books that have been self-published because there are no formal quality checks in place. There are readers who prefer to read a book that's been through a publishing house. My only advice is that you should avoid any vanity publishers that ask you to pay the publication costs. The genuine ones will bear the costs themselves.

What's the difference, you may ask, between a reputable publisher and a vanity publisher? The answer is quite simple. It's a matter of where the profit comes from. A reputable publisher will make a profit by selling books to the general public and a proportion of that profit will go to the writer. Keep in mind that the profit will come from the pockets of the readers who buy those books. A vanity publisher, however, will make his profit entirely from the pocket of the author. It doesn't matter how badly written the book is — and some of them are quite dire — because the vanity publisher will usually take anything that is on offer and has no real incentive to invest much effort into the production process. Good, bad or indifferent, the vanity publisher will offer to publish it entirely at the author's expense. It doesn't matter that not a single copy of the book will be sold, unless the author buys a few copies, because the vanity publisher has already clocked up his profit from the writer's pocket. The message is simple: don't get taken in by vanity publishing; don't pay to have your book published. If it's good enough, a publisher will invest time, effort and money to get it out there into the marketplace.

Self-publishing

That's not such a difficult task with modern technology. You can do everything yourself. Or, you may want to pay for the novel to be professionally edited, and then do the rest of the work yourself. Note that professional editing is a legitimate business and is not the same as vanity publishing. The professional editor will work hard on your manuscript to ensure it is as good as he/she can make it and will want to be paid for that work. As I've already indicated, that editing process will be crucial. Even though you've carefully worked through your manuscript several times, you shouldn't imagine that you've spotted every single minor error. That's most unlikely.

The upside of self-publication is that once your book is out there in the marketplace, every penny of profit from the sales goes to you. You also have complete control over your own work. If you enjoy running a business and want to have more of a say regarding how your book should appear as the end product, this option might be something to consider.

If you decide to take the self-publishing route, there are different ways to do it. Amazon Kindle Direct Publishing (https://kdp.amazon.com) and CreateSpace (www.createspace.com) are services that enable you to reach markets worldwide. I will not go into any details about these here as you can find all the information you need from their websites.

If you want to keep your book publication simple, you could opt for having a few copies printed and give these to your family and friends or sell them at events. This idea is not to be sniffed at. There are amateur writers who craft their novels for their own pleasure, in much the same way amateur painters craft pictures for pleasure. All that matters to such writers is the satisfaction of seeing their novel printed in book form.

This approach is also suitable for public speakers whose talks make a mention of their novel writing and who want to sell a few copies afterwards. If you do no more than sell the books at cost price, it may help get your name better known as a speaker. I have a nephew who was a medical doctor before he went blind. His main interest is poetry and he gives recitals of his work, much of which describes the effects of a blind man living in a seeing world. After his recitals people will usually ask to buy his poems, so he has had a few copies printed for very limited sales.

You can easily upload your manuscript onto a printing website, such as Lulu (www.lulu.com), and a small number of copies can be ordered and produced as and when they are required. The cost is not prohibitive, far less than you would pay a vanity publisher. You will have to format the manuscript, though, but Lulu offers a ready-made template that you can download freely.

Approaching agents and mainstream publishers

Have you made up your mind to approach a literary agent because you want to hit the big time with a major publisher? If so, you now have to sell your novel and sell it hard. How do you go about that? It won't be easy. You've written your novel based upon your 'bright idea'. You've edited it to the best of your ability, but that doesn't automatically mean an agent will take it on. So, how do you make that agent jump for joy when he/she picks up your manuscript?

Let's move away from novels for just one moment. Let's suppose you are in a different business. It's purely hypothetical, but let's suppose the television industry has no sports programmes and you are the first to come along, hoping to sell them a brand new idea. It's a great idea. "Hey, guys," you say, "how about this for a real money earner: You dig a few small holes in the ground, you give a couple of guys some sticks and you get them to hit some balls into those holes. It will make fantastic viewing!" Or, how about this one, "We get these gangs of guys to kick a ball across a field. If they can kick it into a net, the crowds will go wild. Great idea, eh? It'll make millions."

No. Put like that, the big idea isn't likely to work. You see, it's all about *how* you sell the idea. You must put it across in such a way that it becomes supremely attractive.

The way you will sell your idea will be threefold:

1. *A professionally-written cover letter*
2. *An irresistible synopsis*
3. *An eye-catching first chapter*

Taking those three in reverse order, you already have the first chapter, so let's assume it is as good as you can possibly make it. Now you need to prepare a synopsis and a covering letter. And, just for fun, we'll call that accompanying letter a begging letter.

The synopsis

A synopsis is one of those most important items which will help sell your book to a publisher or agent. You will hear people say that it is just a précis of the novel, but it should really be more than that. Much more. A synopsis is what your book is all about. Go back to the starting point for writing your novel. It was the bright spark of an idea that sent you off on the right path. That bright spark should be at the forefront of the synopsis because it is what your book is all about.

In Appendix A, I have shown you the basic ideas from which some of my novels grew. When I came to write the synopses, I went back to those basic ideas. So, go and find the notes you made when you decided upon your basic idea. In a tidied up form, they will be at the heart of your synopsis.

A word of warning here: Don't confuse the words 'synopsis' and 'blurb'. The synopsis needs to include the ending where-as the blurb, the bit on the back cover of a book, is aimed at customers who mustn't know the ending in advance.

You won't actually need a synopsis when you write the book, but an agent or publisher most certainly will want to see one when you submit. Agents in particular are inundated with work from hopeful writers. They don't have time to read every complete manuscript in order to determine how the plot pans out, so they'll rely upon your synopsis to tell them. If they like the idea and they like the opening page, they'll read on. If they decide the idea is old hat and/or the writing is mundane, they'll toss it aside and read the next offering. You've got to get past that hurdle, so your synopsis has to be as enticing as your first page. It must shine.

It isn't an easy task, so be prepared to take some time over it. Think back to those four questions I put to you when you were fleshing out your basic idea. You can use the answers to those questions here.

1. *Who is the main character in this story?* In other words, who is this novel about? We must know this right at the start. Some writers like to use bold or capital letters when first mentioning the name of the main character(s) in a synopsis.

2. *What is that character's problem?* What is the conflict that your main character faces, the problem that makes the story work?

3. *What's preventing a quick solution?* In a short story, the problem may be solved within the space of a few hundred words. What is it about the problem in the novel that makes it more difficult to solve? What is it that demands one hundred thousand words or so to find a solution?

4. *How does it all pan out in the end?* In very brief terms, how does the main character win through in the end? The synopsis must tell us how the story ends because the agent will want to know that you have devised a logical and satisfying conclusion.

The person who reads your synopsis — the agent or publisher — will want clear answers to those questions, usually in 500 to 700 words. Busy agents and publishers don't have time to wade through lengthy and highly-detailed synopses, so keep it manageable. If you can provide satisfactory answers to those questions, the next one will be: What is it about your novel that makes it stand out from the crowd? And that's the killer question, so you'd better think about it carefully.

This is the opening of a synopsis for one of my novels. I will not give you the full synopsis because I don't want to spoil the ending for a potential reader.

My name
Address
Email
Telephone number

The Legacy of Shame
by
David Hough
A contemporary adventure
32 chapters
120,000 words

Synopsis:

The Legacy of Shame *is a contemporary story of* ***Faith Rivers****, a girl who has grown up in a tribal community in the Amazon rainforest. Knowing she does not belong there, she is determined to find her way to the outside world. The novel focuses on Faith's escape from the jungle and the outcome of her search for her roots.*

The novel begins with ***Bridget Hadleigh****, Faith's birth-mother, who lives in England, now married to a man who is not Faith's father. Their home is thrown into turmoil when a letter from Australia arrives out of the blue. Faith has made her way to the antipodes, discovered something of her past and now wants to make contact with Bridget.*

Faith eventually meets her birth-mother and relates the story of her years of growing up in the jungle. That revelation is the highly emotional centrepiece of the novel. Bridget's reaction to the tale is less than accommodating. She does not want to tell Faith the story behind her birth.

As I said, that's just the opening to my synopsis, but it gives you an idea of how you can tell an agent, in outline, what the story is all about.

How did I answer the killer question?

Like this:

The Legacy of Shame *differs from other reconciliation stories in two ways:*

1. It plumbs the depth of anguish which all the main characters suffer. In particular, it reaches deep into the souls of Faith Rivers and Bridget Hadleigh as they struggle to come to terms with a real and unpalatable truth: that a forced adoption harmed both of them.

2. It goes beyond the harsh reality of girls who became pregnant in Catholic Ireland in the 1960s. It looks into the experiences of those who were forced to leave their homes in disgrace and ended up in Australia. There, the state illegally took away their babies at birth because they were deemed unfit to be mothers.

Did the story plumb such depths of emotion? Well, one reviewer wrote: "It will break your heart and open your mind." And that was the effect I set out to explore.

In summary, a synopsis should:

- *be around 500 to 700 words long, i.e. between one and two pages*

- *summarise your plot completely, including the ending*
- *spell out what makes you novel stand out from the crowd*
- *make clear who your main characters are*
- *be written in a clear, business-like style*
- *be well presented, single-spaced and typed in a clear font*

The synopsis should *not:*

- *go into great detail about the characters or the setting*
- *relate minor aspects of the story or subplots*
- *leave the agent or publisher guessing about how it all pans out in the end*

Having said this, always check the agent's/publisher's submission advice and style guidelines, and follow them meticulously.

The begging letter

Now let's go back a step to the letter that accompanies your submission. The expression 'begging letter' is just a bit of humour. You're not going to get down on your hands and knees and plead with an agent or publisher to take you on — of course not. That would be demeaning. Instead, you're going to write a carefully constructed covering letter which will introduce your masterpiece. I like to think of it as a well-phrased begging letter, not entirely unlike the charity letters that pour through your letter box with every postal delivery. They are professionally written to pull at your heart strings.

If you prefer, you can think of the letter as a sales pitch. You're trying to sell your masterpiece and, strange as it may seem, you're also trying to sell yourself as a writer. "Look at me," you'll be saying (but not literally) in that letter. "I've written a wonderful novel and now I want to offer it to you. You can't afford to pass up this offer."

Well, actually, they can. So you're going to have to make your pitch stand out from the crowd. If you want an agent to invest time, money and effort in your book, you'll also have to appeal to their good nature within that letter. Don't even think of trying a self-satisfied proclamation of the wonderful merits of your manuscript, coupled with overdone reasons why it cannot be passed over. That will not do the trick. Your begging letter will have to be very subtle indeed.

Here is an example of how a begging letter might look:

Dear Aggie Read,

I enclose for your consideration a synopsis and three chapters of my 120,000-word novel titled *The Legacy of Shame*.

The Legacy of Shame is the story of a girl who has grown up in the Amazon rainforest, knowing she does not belong there. The story follows her search for her roots in the outside world.

The Legacy of Shame is my third novel. The previous two were published by Robert Hale.

I look forward to your response.

Yours sincerely

David Hough

David Hough

How to publicise your book

If you get a contract and your book is published, be prepared to get involved in the publicising of your novel. Years ago a publisher looked after all that. Today, things are different. Even if you are taken on board by a mainstream publisher, you will be expected to do much of the publicity work.

For a start, you will need a website and you will need a presence on social networking sites (e.g. Facebook and/or Twitter). You will have to be prepared to talk about your book and make yourself known to various media outlets, such as radio and newspapers. I have given talks to library reading groups and writing groups. I have written articles for various magazines and used the internet (including Facebook and my website www.thenovelsofdavidhough.com) to promote my work. On one occation, I drove one hundred miles just to get myself onto an hour-long BBC radio programme. You should be prepared to put in at least that degree of effort if you plan to self-publish your work.

The downside is that the more time you spend seeking publicity, the less time you will have for writing your next novel — but the publicity trail is one that you must be prepared to follow.

If your novel is published and is out there in the big wide world, people are going to talk about it. Some will like it and some will not, so you may need to develop a thick skin. The chances are your book is going to be reviewed. Some reviews will be kind and others will be cruel. Get used to that idea. It's going to be the reality of your writing life.

Among your family and friends you will be viewed as 'a writer' and writers are always fair game for criticism. Yes, even among family and friends. It goes with the job. There will be times when you will be pleased with the feedback you get; at other times you will have to be very patient and tactful. I recall a party at which I was approached by a man who had written one novel. I'd read it in full and judged that no publisher would ever be likely to accept it. It was that bad. I made no critical comments as I didn't want to upset him. He, however, spent some time giving me the benefit of his 'expert' opinion on my writing. That included telling me, rather pointedly, that I had got things wrong with my latest (published with good reviews) book. I had to use the utmost patience and tact in steering the conversation around to something quite different.

There's an important message here. You must never rise to the bait of an ill-informed critic, especially in public. If you want to sell your books, you will need to be seen by everyone as the reader's friend, the sort of person anyone would be happy to sit down with and enjoy a friendly chat over a cup of tea. Being nice to your readers also increases the chances of them coming back to buy your next book.

THE SUMMARY

Well done on reaching this point in the book.

At the start, I told you I would describe a way of writing a novel that would maximise your chance of success and minimise your chance of ending up in tears. I said it was based upon a very simple system, which I call the Waypoint Method. It's a system that has worked well for me and enabled me to complete more than thirty novels, all of which have been taken up by publishers.

Here's a checklist of the different stages of novel writing which I have described in this book:

- Start with a bright idea — without that idea, you have no foundation on which to build your novel.
- Flesh out the idea into a plot — fleshing out the story is akin to adding meat to the bare bones with which you began. It gives your novel the feeling of substance.
- Create the main characters — it is vitally important that your characters are suitably designed to fit into your plot.
- Create the setting
- Plan the chapters — bring the plot and the characters together and work out how you're going to tell your story. In other words, create your route map.
- Write the first chapter

- Write the ending
- Write the waypoint chapters
- Write the bits in between
- Prime-edit your novel
- Copy-edit your novel
- Send your novel out to the world
- Be prepared to publicise your book to the best of your ability

Thank you for reading this book. I hope it has been of use to you, and I wish you well in your future career as a novel writer.

QUESTIONS AND ANSWERS

Over the years I have been asked a lot of questions about the process of novel writing. Here are some of the answers I have given.

How much planning should I do before I start writing?

If you want to follow my example, you should plan, plan and plan again until you are quite sure that the story will work. Then start on Chapter 1. My way works for me; however, I respect the fact that some writers (the ones we call pantsers) do far less planning. Some do none at all. If the pantsers' way works for you, stick with it, but beware of the pitfalls.

Do I need to have the whole plot figured out before I start writing?

Yes, if you are a planner like me. I could never have completed more than thirty novels if I didn't do it this way. It's the only way for me to avoid that thing known as writer's block. Remember that maxim I mentioned earlier in the book: if you don't know where you are going, you will never know when you arrive. I always know where my story is going and I know exactly when I reach the final dénouement.

How much do I need to know about my characters before I start writing?

More than you will use in your story. Good planners will know their main characters inside out before they start on Chapter 1. They will know exactly how their characters will react in the circumstances created for them. Most importantly, the characters' reactions and behaviour will always be consistent with their personality. In an odd moment, when you are doing nothing else, why not construct a life history for your main character? Jot down everything about his life so far and have that information beside you when you begin to draft your story.

Can the character flaws be something that aren't inherently bad?

Of course. A key character should always be human and that means being flawed because no one is perfect. Your protagonist will most likely have flaws that are not inherently bad. Your villain, however, will more likely be at the opposite end of the scale.

How do I decide upon the best setting for my novel?

If you begin with the bright idea, the setting should naturally develop from it. As you're constructing your plot, consider what kind of setting would enhance the conflict in your story. Or choose your setting based on the mood or atmosphere it adds to your plot: for example, a cosy romance could be set in a vicarage in St Mary Mead and a murder mystery could take place in Chicago gangster-land. So, think about your bright idea first and then look for a setting that enhances your plot. Problems with regard to the setting will more likely arise where the writer starts on Chapter 1 without first defining the sort of story he/she wants to write.

How do I overcome writer's block?

As I related earlier in this book, I have only once experienced that thing they call writer's block. At least, I assume that is what it was. It happened because I had not planned the story and my characters were not designed to take the plot where it seemed to be going. I met a brick wall with no clear way out. I had to start again. From there on I became a committed planner. Nowadays, I always know exactly what is going to happen next so I am never faced with an insoluble problem. Follow the advice in this book and you too can be free of the thing they call writer's block.

I don't have a lot of free time. Is there any point in even starting to write a novel?

Of course there is — if you really want to write a novel. You say you don't have a lot of free time, but I suggest you can conjure up the odd hour or two when you could be working on a novel. When you are on the bus or train, travelling to work, or when you're having lunch, you could be thinking about your story and your characters. Take a notebook or electronic device with you and jot down your ideas as they occur. Once those notes show promise, your enthusiasm will rise up sufficiently to make you find the time needed to start the actual writing process.

We all have to make choices about how we use our time. If you really want to write a novel, it helps to rethink your priorities. Do you really have to watch TV when there's nothing worth watching? Do you really have to spend so much time on social media? If you feel that time is slipping through your fingers, take out your diary and block out some writing time — and stick to your plan.

In my experience, people who tell me, "I don't have the time," are more often than not using that as an excuse to avoid writing. If you find yourself using this sentence a lot, do some soul-searching and see if the real reason for 'not having time' is actually fear (more specifically, the fear of the unknown). It is perfectly understandable to feel fear, but it doesn't have to mean that you can't write a novel. If you follow the advice in this book, you can reduce the fear of the unknown — and you can write that novel.

I have heard some people say that the best way to learn to write is to read novels by authors you admire and not study novel writing guides. What's your view?

Read both. Read the writing guides in order to learn the techniques of writing. The novels will not teach you that. Read the novels in order to develop your preferred style of writing. That will come through as a process of osmosis while you enjoy the authors' way of putting across their stories.

How many words should my novel have?

As many as it needs to tell the story, but new writers are advised to aim at somewhere between 70,000 and 90,000 words. That's the sort of length a publisher would prefer. However, when you are as rich and famous as J.K. Rowling, you can ignore that advice and write to whatever length you wish.

I have written a fantasy novel that is just over 400,000 words. Is this too long?

Yes, especially if you are a new writer. The publisher is, in the first instance, taking a bit of a chance on you and will not want to over-commit on the financial investment. It costs more for the publisher to push out a two-inch thick book than a one-inch thick one. Keep you manuscript within the 70-90,000 word limit and you'll have a better chance of success.

I would like to include a prologue in my novel. Any advice?

I'm not entirely enthusiastic about prologues although I have used them. The trouble is that writers tend to like them — I don't know why — but readers often skim over them or disregard them completely. That's why some publishers dislike them. They can be effective in the right circumstances, of course, but are you sure that a prologue will be right for your novel?

So, what are the right circumstances? Well, let me give you an example. Imagine a crime story which begins with a girl on her way home from school. She says goodbye to her friends as she gets off the school bus, but she never arrives home. No one knows what has happened to her. That's the prologue, short and simple. Chapter 1 starts ten years later when a body is discovered... and the rest of the book is about the task of finding the killer.

That prologue would work, but many prologues could just as easily be incorporated into the first chapter... or scrapped completely. If you really must use one, keep it short and be absolutely sure that it can't be tackled in any other way.

How do I know when I have edited my novel enough?

Put it away for a month. Then come back to it and read it again. If you cannot find one single flaw in it, it's ready to go to the agent or publisher.

I sent my manuscript to an agent six months ago, but I haven't heard anything. How long should I wait until I can send it to another agent?

After six months, I suggest you send in a short, polite email asking if the agent has received your submission. I would also try other agents in the meantime. As I've said earlier, it's worth submitting your manuscript to several agents at once so that you're not left waiting around in case an agent never bothers to reply.

What's the best writing advice that you've ever been given?

Write only what genuinely interests you, regardless of what other people want. If you enjoy the subject, your passion is likely to show through. If you write a story because someone else thought it would be a good idea, your story is likely to be lacking in that essential passion. In other words, be true to yourself and your particular literary love. The techniques of writing can be learned; the passion for the subject cannot.

APPENDICES

APPENDIX A
PRACTICAL EXAMPLES OF BRIGHT IDEAS

Here are some practical examples of how I began my novels with a spark of inspiration and how another writer might pick up ideas in a similar way.

1. Responding to someone else's thoughts or comments

How I did it

The Legacy of Shame, my first successful full-length novel, stemmed from a 1,000-word short story. It told of a child in a South American rainforest tribe, cast out because she didn't belong there. The story won the second prize in a competition. Later the adjudicator gave me his own thoughts about the story. He told me he wanted to know what happened next. How did the girl get there in the first place? Where did she go? Did she find her real home and family? It was those questions which gave me the 'bright idea' for the full-length novel.

How someone else might do it

It's lunch time in the works canteen. The writer is chatting to a colleague who tells her about a story she has just read in a magazine. It's a sad tale about a woman who spent years looking after a sick husband. Now widowed, she has trouble trying to find someone else to share her life with. The writer's colleague comments that the woman should have started looking when her husband was still alive. "It would have made the transition so much easier," she says. How callous, the writer thinks, but then she wonders just how it might have worked out. Maybe... and the thought suddenly comes to her... maybe she could have had her dying husband's support. Is there a story here waiting to be told? It could be a very emotional tale.

2. Responding to someone's anecdote

How I did it

Prestwick is one of my more popular novels. The idea behind it came from my working life as an air traffic controller. One day a colleague called by for a cup of coffee and a chat, and he told me how two aircraft had come too close over the North Atlantic. The crew of one aircraft had set the wrong coordinates into their flight management computer. No harm came to anyone on board either flight, but the anecdote intrigued me. It became the basic premise out of which I created the novel. I asked myself, "What if they had actually collided?" and there it was: the spark of an idea.

How someone else might do it

A writer is having a cup of coffee with an old friend. In the course of conversation, the friend launches into a description of why her latest date doesn't quite tick all the right boxes. "Would you believe," she says, "I thought he was absolutely perfect, and then I caught him phoning another woman. 'Remember all the good times we had together,' he said to the other woman. Naturally, I dumped him like a hot potato."

It's the end of a relationship for the friend, but a story idea for the writer. She takes a moment to think of all the reasons why the boyfriend might have been phoning another woman. Good ones and bad ones. She might have been his mother, or sister... or first love. There's the germ of a relationship story hiding in there, something a writer can pick up and develop into a story.

3. Being inspired by non-fiction books

How I did it

The Legacy of Secrets, one of my longer novels, stemmed from reading a non-fiction book which went into the subject of reincarnation. The book posed some interesting questions, such as: Why would souls come back in later lives? What are they trying to achieve? That set me thinking.

The novel started with the basic idea of a young man troubled with nightmare scenes of events he could not possible have experienced in his present life. He knows he must learn something from those nightmares. But what? Did those dreams link back to a previous life? Well, that's how the idea began.

How someone else might do it

A writer has just finished reading a book about past lives in which one woman claims to have been burned as a witch in the Middle Ages. She begins to wonder what the historical woman did that caused people to claim she was a witch. Could she have been a healer who understood natural remedies better than anyone and used them to cure the apparently incurable? Could she have put together a book of natural cures that would set the medical world afire if it could be found today? That might be an idea for a story.

4. Latching on to a subject of a lesson or an interesting teaching point

How I did it

The Legacy of Conflict began as a teaching point which a creative writing instructor put across in a class. "Your characters must change in the course of the story," she told us. "They must learn something from their experience and grow in maturity as a result." That gave me my basic idea, and I was quickly fired up to take it to an extreme. Could I begin the story with a character who appeared totally and utterly unlikeable? Could I then develop and change that character (or the reader's perception of that character) into the real hero or heroine of the plot? That was the basic concept from which the novel developed.

How someone else might do it

A creative writing instructor is teaching his class to 'show not tell'. "Imagine a girl has been jilted at the altar," he says.

"Don't tell us she's upset. Ask yourself: How would she show her feelings? What would she do to express her intense emotional pain?" That gives one of the class members an idea. Suppose the jilted bride, in her distress, immediately ran from the church and threw herself in front of a car. She would be injured, but her life would be saved by a junior doctor from among the wedding guests.

And there is yet another basic idea, one that could be taken forward to any conclusion the writer chose.

5. A story set around a proverb, saying or maxim

How I did it

The plot for *In the Shadow of a Curse* arose from the premise that you can run from a place but you can't run from a curse. It's a historical novel in which I set out to show how a man trying to escape a shaman's curse finds that running away from it doesn't work. He must face up to his demons. The rest followed from that basic concept.

How someone else might do it

There's no fool like an old fool, so it's said. What ideas does that conjure up? How about the story of an elderly widower apparently conned out of his life savings by a much younger woman who persuades him into an unwise relationship? His son decides to take revenge and get the money back, but he doesn't reckon on the woman turning her sights onto him. Okay, there's the idea; all it needs is the process of development.

6. Taking an alternative viewpoint to an existing story

How I did it

The idea for *In the Shadow of Disgrace* came, surprisingly, from reading Daphne du Maurier's *Jamaica Inn*. Du Maurier had a female protagonist drawn into the smuggling activities of a male character. I turned that on its head and had a male protagonist drawn into the world of a female Cornish smuggler. A simple change, and yet it gave me a novel that is nothing like Du Maurier's story.

How someone else might do it

The story in the film *Saving Private Ryan* is seen from an American viewpoint. They are the good guys and the Germans are the bad guys. It's a great movie, as one would expect from Spielberg. But, just suppose a keen writer watches that film and then wonders if there might be an alternative story? Something that has rarely been tackled: the German viewpoint. Suppose, he wonders, the key character is a German officer and Private Ryan (the name would have to change) is a war criminal. Both sides want him, but for different reasons. How would that translate into a novel?

7. Researching local or national history

How I did it

I was born in Cornwall, a place of legend and fascinating history. When I came to write *In the Shadow of a Curse*, I had a clear aim in mind: to write a story about life in 19th century Cornwall. I borrowed library books, downloaded information from the internet and, most importantly, I visited again the very places where the story would be set. The research threw up many ideas for the story. I was forced to throw aside most of them, but I may well use them at a later date.

How someone else might do it

Let's suppose our writer is an Irishman who has been researching the story of the Viking king called Magnus Barelegs. Conventional history shows the Vikings as invaders, but our writer decides to look deeper into history. He discovers Barelegs, who was killed in Ireland, was the victim of a treacherous conspiracy. That becomes the basic idea, and all it needs is the process of development to turn it into a novel.

8. What did my favourite author(s) write?

How I did it

I have a great admiration for the books of Dashiell Hammett and Raymond Chandler and I wanted to write a series of novels in a style they might use if they were alive today. That was my starting point, my basic idea: to write gritty crime stories in the style of an American pulp fiction writer. In the event, I wrote four murder-mystery novels under a '*Death in...*' banner. Hammett and Chandler had their private eye investigators, but I decided against that. I chose to have an amateur looking into the murders I dreamed up. He would be an American airline pilot who would have the misfortune to run into devious deeds wherever he went. It was a simple concept that began with *Death in Ireland* and continued with *Death in France*, *Death in England* and *Death in Scotland*.

How someone else might do it

Jane Austen's works are still widely read and translated into successful films. A writer who admires Austen's work might decide to tackle the sort of book she would create if she were alive today. It would have to be written in modern language, of course, and would require modern settings, but it would centre upon those very things Austen wrote about: manners, relationships, families and, most importantly, people and their foibles.

This much has been done before, of course, so where does the new idea come from? What aspect of today's life is markedly different from Jane Austen's life, but would merit a Jane Austen approach? How about taking a new angle on Elizabeth Bennet? Instead of her ups-and-downs relationship with Mr Darcy, could she have a similar experience with Ms Darcy? The heir to a grand country manor, Ms Darcy, could appear to have a very proud attitude, and a prejudiced view of the way Elizabeth leads her life. Okay? Take it from there.

APPENDIX B
MORE EXAMPLES OF HOW TO FLESH OUT THE BASIC IDEAS

If you're struggling with the fleshing out process, here are two more examples of how I did it.

Example 1: Prestwick — an aviation thriller

The basic idea involved two aircraft colliding over the North Atlantic. I had to ask myself several important plotting questions. Firstly, which aircraft were involved? Secondly, why did they collide? Thirdly, what additional problems could I throw at the crews? And, fourthly, who else would be caught up in the excitement?

The answers came quite logically. I chose to make one aircraft a civil airliner with four hundred people on board because that would give me ample scope for panic in the passenger cabin. I then chose to make the second aircraft a military tanker because it would have huge fuel tanks inside the fuselage — an ideal ploy to keep the reader wondering if it was going to explode. The reason for the collision was relatively easy. One crew was overly tired and fell asleep — yes, it does happen — and the pilot of the other aircraft made a fundamental error of navigation. So far, so good. I wrote all that down in brief outline form, handwritten notes jotted down in my scribble book.

Now, what about a few additional problems? Suppose the pilot is caught up in something illegal and that's why he was distracted when he fed in the flight coordinates. Yes, I could make something of that. And what about a few problems on the ground? Suppose the weather is so bad that there is only one airfield open and... ah, yes, this sounds good...
suppose the airfield controller refuses landing permission because of an even greater emergency. I'll work out what that other emergency is later. For now, I'm onto a roll. I can begin to think about the other people involved, like the ground controllers. Yes, I can have some fun with them, especially if one of them makes things even worse.

I wrote down all these ideas as no more than scrappy handwritten jottings. It didn't matter if I was the only one who could understand those notes because no one else was going to read them. The idea behind the novel was now starting to take shape. It had been fleshed out into something that could be woven into a viable story.

Example 2: The Legacy of Conflict — historical mystery

The Legacy of Conflict began as an exercise in creating a character who would change (or be perceived to change) dramatically as the story unfolded. I quickly realised that there had to be a likeable character in the story, someone the unlikeable character could use as a whipping boy (or girl), someone to be taunted and who would get upset. I had to create two people, one relatively stable and the other emotionally unstable. I decided on two young women, twins who were parted in early life. They would meet again when they were around twenty years old. They had to come from dramatically different backgrounds. I settled for one growing up in an affluent environment in the south of England and the other growing up in relative poverty, in a deprived area of Belfast. I've lived in both places and could describe them in detail from my own experience. The southern English girl would be rather prim and proper. The Irish twin would be the one with the emotional problems, the one who would change as the plot progressed, the one who would become the ultimate heroine.

It sounded like I had a basic idea that would work, so I jotted down my fleshed-out ideas in a notebook, ready for the next stage of development.

APPENDIX C
THINGS TO LOOK OUT FOR WHILE COPY-EDITING

Grammar and the correct use of words

Read through the following text and see how much of the grammar needs changing.

I only knew a fraction of what she had been up to and I wanted to know lots more. I decided to look at her Facebook account, but it was all rubbish and I soon got bored of it. Where else could I look? I had three alternatives up my sleeve. Firstly, there was her diary. When I read the opening page, I literally jumped out of my skin. What should I do? Should I pretend I never read it, wait for an opportunity to ask her about it, or confront her straight away? It was a dilemma.

Let's take the first half of that paragraph:

I only knew a fraction of what she had been up to and I wanted to know lots more. I decided to look at her Facebook account, but it was all rubbish and I soon got bored of it.

I only knew — This should read: *I knew only...* because we are looking at what the 'I' character knew... i.e. he knew *only a fraction...*

A fraction — A fraction can be big or small. This needs an adjective... e.g. a *small* fraction

Bored — You get bored *with* something, not *of* it.

Now let's look at the second half of the paragraph:

Where else could I look? I had three alternatives up my sleeve. Firstly, there was her diary. When I read the opening page, I literally jumped out of my skin. What should I do? Should I pretend I never read it, wait for an opportunity to ask her about it, or confront her straight away? It was a dilemma.

Alternatives — There can only ever be two alternatives. Three or more are 'options'.

I literally jumped out of my skin. — A silly statement. No one can literally jump out of their skin.

Straight away — Depending on your particular style, you could say that this should be written straightaway.

Comma after 'it' — Again, depending on your particular style, it could be argued that the comma shouldn't be there.

Dilemma — A dilemma (from the Greek meaning 'two propositions') can only be between two alternatives. Anything else is a problem or a quandary.

Collective nouns

This subject is a cause of frequent errors. Have a look at the next sentence and see if you can spot what is wrong with it.

> *"The crowd of protesters are all dispersed now," the policeman said.*

What's wrong with that, you may ask. If you don't get it immediately, try working out what's wrong with this next sentence.

> *"A shoal of piranha are attacking him!" she cried.*

Get it now?

The problem here lies in the use of what we call *collective nouns*. These are words that group together more than one person, animal, place or thing under the auspices of one word. For example *team* is a word covering a number of players. Team is a collective noun. *Family* is a group of people who are related. So, *family* is a collective noun.

Each collective noun can be singular or plural. If singular, it attracts singular pronouns and singular verbs. If the collective noun is plural, it attracts plural pronouns and plural verbs. So, what makes the collective noun singular or plural?

It all depends upon the context in which it occurs, and whether the group acts in the same way (as a unified group) or in differing ways (as a gathering of individuals each doing his or her own thing).

Let's look at a couple of examples.

> *The writing class was so delighted when the teacher brought in some cake that it broke into a round of applause.*

In this context, *class* is a singular collective noun encompassing a uniform group of writers all doing the same thing. *Was so delighted* is singular because the group acted in unison. Additionally, *it* is a singular pronoun. It refers to the one group, not the various individuals within the group.

Compare that with this example:

> *The writing class started work on their individual writing projects. They scratched diligently at their notebooks, sighed or gazed around the room as the fancy took them.*

In this context, the word *class* is a plural collective noun. It refers to a group who are doing different things. Some are writing diligently, some are sighing and some are gazing around the room. They are still a class, but they are not acting in unison. *They* and *them* are plural pronouns.

Now go back to the first two examples and see if you can spot what is wrong.

Make each word pull its weight

The following paragraph is far too weighty. See if you can shorten it to give it more punch.

It felt utterly frightening when she went up one of those long stairways that seemed to go nowhere until you get to the top and then you realise it probably wasn't where you meant to go anyway, which we all do now and again. There was another big corridor going off in one direction, a really long one, and it didn't look like it was what she was looking for so she turned round and went back down the first stairway until she was at the bottom again and then she gave a sigh of relief.

This can be shortened to:

Fear gripped her as she climbed the long stairway. She paused at the top step and looked along the corridor. Was this the right place?

It felt wrong. She turned and rushed back down the stairs.

Clichés

What do we mean by a cliché? Well, look at these two definitions from the Oxford English Dictionary:

Cliché — a hackneyed phrase or opinion
Hackneyed — made commonplace or trite by long overuse

By definition, a cliché is something hackneyed, commonplace or trite. Is that how you want your writing to be seen? Do you want your readers to think of your writing as hackneyed, commonplace or trite? Of course not. You want your writing to come across as fresh and original. The only time you should use a cliché is when it occurs in the dialogue of a character with limited vocabulary. It then becomes a part of that character's personality.

How many clichés can you count in the following paragraph?

Sarah trotted along the road without a care in the world. She thought she had nerves of steel. Even her boyfriend, Billy, said she was brave as a lion and he had never been scared out of his wits. But it was only a matter of time before Sarah would be frightened to death. When she had to face her worst fears, it was Billy who saved her in the nick of time.

In fact, there are eight:

Sarah trotted along the road <u>without a care in the world</u>. She thought she had <u>nerves of steel</u>. Even her boyfriend, Billy, said she was <u>brave as a lion</u> and he had never been <u>scared out of his wits</u>. But it was only <u>a matter of time</u> before Sarah would be <u>frightened to death</u>. When she had to <u>face her worst fears</u>, it was Billy who saved her <u>in the nick of time</u>.

Repeated words

This is another extract from that non-existent novel I mentioned earlier, *A Night with a Knight*. Look at the number of words that are repeated:

Sir Jasper stared at me with a wide-awake look in his eyes.

"Aha! So you're awake me dear," he said.

The bed's well-worn springs squealed as I sat up in the bed. "Of course I'm awake, and you're looking sprightly, sir," I said.

"As sprightly as ever and we've more business ahead of us, ain't we?" he said. "Come 'ere, girl. Let's get down to business again."

"Oh, sir," I squealed as he wrapped his arms around me and...

If you have the same word twice (or more) in fairly quick succession, it can look a little clumsy. Watch out for any words that you've repeated, and look for a synonym to replace it. Don't worry about extremely common words like 'the' or, in dialogue, 'said' — those won't stand out.

THE WORKBOOK

Did you know that there is a workbook to complement this novel writing guide? It's called:

A ROUTE MAP TO NOVEL WRITING SUCCESS: THE WORKBOOK
A practical aid to using the Waypoint Method

It's not essential to use this workbook in order to write a successful novel, but it will almost certainly help. This is what the workbook contains:

- Checklists to help you keep track of your overall progress
- Summary pages that you can use as a quick reference when you start writing your novel
- Prompts to help you think of and decide upon your bright idea
- Prompts to flesh out your bright idea into a plot
- Prompts to help you develop your characters and setting
- Guidance for putting your chapters together, including a grid to help you plan those chapters
- Space to explore your novel's title and the all-important first sentence
- Space to explore your own writing style and the right point of view for your novel
- Space for jotting down expressions, descriptions, snippets of dialogue and other turns of phrase
- Space to record your research findings and references
- Space to record potential agents'/publishers' contact details and their submission guidelines
- Guidance for writing your synopsis and cover letter
- Space for your own notes

22499686R00097

Printed in Great Britain
by Amazon